W9-BMN-945

Sinai Temple: A Centennial History

1906–2006

WRITTEN BY
Florie Brizel

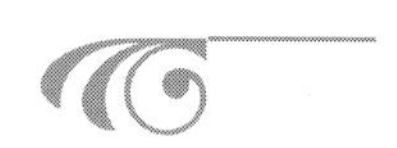

Brina Rosenbaum, Publisher

Sinai Temple: A Centennial History

An Ellen Schneid Coleman Literary Services Production

Cover and Interior Design: Thomas Nery

Composition: Inkwell Publishing Services

Printed in the United States of America

15 14 13 12 11 10 09 08 07 1 2 3 4 5

Library of Congress Control Number: 2007921584

ISBN: 978-0-9792855-0-9
0-9792855-0-X

www.sinaitemple.org

Table of Contents

"Man is a builder, and as a builder is the noblest of God's creations...he adds love to a house and calls it a home; he adds learning to a pile of bricks and calls it a school; he adds compassion to a city and calls it a community; and he adds religion to the edifice and calls it a sanctuary. He adds brotherhood of man and the fatherhood of God, and this is the ultimate path of his ideal vision. Man may never complete what he builds, but the collective building by his fellowmen completes the edifice. The builder of today builds unaware into the temple of the future."

Rabbi Israel Chodos

Foreword

The future is created by an alliance of our history and our dreams. Too often we know only our dreams. Yet without understanding what has gone before we are lost in the moment, without foundation, without perspective, without the wisdom that the past can proffer.

One hundred years is a brief flash in the history of the Jewish people, but for an American synagogue it is a long time indeed. The founders of Sinai were mindful of tradition. They knew that without dedication to preserve what is precious, Judaism crumbles. Yet they were also committed to creating something new: We are at once an eternal and ever changing people; that recognition stands at the center of Conservative Judaism. Through its passion, creativity, and learning, Sinai stands at the forefront of a Judaism that can both integrate and shape the modern world. Vision and memory together make the Conservative movement and Sinai Temple indispensable to the Jewish mission.

This history, lovingly crafted, full of fascinating information and remarkable individuals, is a testament to the foresight of the generations. "For you shall inquire of the past, of the days before your own" (Deuteronomy 4:32). You hold history in your hands. May it inspire all of us to carry on the work of those who have gone before, to honor them and to serve God.

Rabbi David Wolpe

Preface

Three years ago, during my term as president of Sinai, the Temple initiated plans for its Centennial Celebration. I began our history project with the goal of creating a book that would factually reflect temple records, as well as the memories of members, their descendents, and staff. With a great love for our *shul*, having dedicated over 30 years to Sinai with my husband and family, I was eager to begin.

After assessing the needs of the overall project and creating a budget, I hired Florie Brizel, a talented writer, and Ellen Schneid Coleman, an editor with impeccable credentials. In order to uncover the temple's rich history, Florie conducted interviews with a cross-section of individuals who provided us with personal views of the past including priceless stories and anecdotes. We supplemented interviews with field trips to Sinai's previous locations and spent countless hours researching and reviewing Temple documents. Florie also became familiar with life at Sinai by attending services, meetings, and programs.

To my surprise, we faced a large roadblock at the start of the project—there were no central archives! In searching the temple, we found everything scattered, from the wall room above the main sanctuary to the organ room in the lower garage. Our discoveries included a multitude of treasures, including old and crumbling handwritten documents and photographs that lay forgotten in dusty file cabinets. It therefore became important to create central archives in order to organize and preserve the materials, so we looked for an unused location in the building, requisitioned file cabinets and desks, and gathered and sorted files, board minutes, correspondence, and photographs in one enclosed area.

Researching, managing, and pre-editing the book over these past three years have helped me to appreciate—on a profound level—the congregation's past 100 years. Sinai has faced enormous challenges, yet, through the vision of our leadership and the dedication of our members, we have grown, flourished, and helped to

meet the needs of the Los Angeles Jewish Community while preserving and enhancing its role in the Conservative movement.

I sincerely thank the people who contributed to the production of this book, from those who provided their memories, to those who provided their mementos, to those who provided their assistance and support: you have made this book possible. My personal thanks to: Doris Siegel of blessed memory, for her sage advice, wise counsel, and for sharing the unwritten stories as only she could tell them; Penny Dain, Sinai's Public Relations Coordinator, for her gracious assistance with photos and printed material; my daughter, Dr. Deborah Rosenbaum Smith, for a prepublication critique of the manuscript; my parents, Fannie and Harry Chananie of blessed memory, for modeling their lifelong commitment to Judaism; Phil, Sharon, Mark, Jordan, Tyler, and Harry for their inspiration.

Special thanks to Rabbi David Wolpe, Rabbi David Lieber, Tom Flesh, Rita Frischer, Dr. Ed Kamenir, Mark Haloossim, Dr. Julius Lesner, Ovvie Miller, Jerry Nagin, Gordon M. Smith, and Anna Tenenblatt, who took the time to read and comment on the manuscript. With great pleasure, we have included many of their valuable suggestions.

I am privileged to provide you with our Centennial History. Enjoy!

BRINA ROSENBAUM
President, Sinai Temple 2003–2005

Serving as president of our wonderful congregation is an honor and a joy. And now I have the added pleasure of greeting you and introducing this beautiful commemorative of our Centennial Celebration. We should all feel proud that we helped create this magical place. A special thank you to Brina Rosenbaum for her tireless work these past few years in creating this book. I hope that it continues to remind us of our achievements and of the work we have yet to do.

Tom Flesh

The entrance to 12th and Valencia (recent photo)

Chapter One

Wandering Jews

Jews who made the hazardous trek to the wilds of the West Coast in the early 1900s—sometimes by choice, sometimes by necessity—left behind almost everything familiar, hoping to make a better life. Most of them had migrated from two distinct regions in the world: back East (anywhere east of the Mississippi) or Europe, including Russia. Many came for economic opportunity. Many others came for a better climate to improve their poor health.

The majority of Jews moving west initially moved to San Francisco; their first documented arrival in Southern California occurred in 1841. By 1885, Congregation B'nai B'rith, an Orthodox synagogue, opened its doors for worship. Today this is the Reform congregation Wilshire Boulevard Temple.

At the turn of the 20th century, approximately 2,500 Jews lived in Southern California. Then, the 1906 earthquake in San Francisco killed nearly 1,000 people and rattled the nerves of survivors, prompting many more to head south to Los Angeles in the last great quest for land ownership and development.

By all accounts, early Jewish Angelenos worked in all sectors of the burgeoning economy, from farming to factories. They integrated easily into mainstream gentile society until 1891, when the mostly Protestant community began to exclude them from previously mixed events and environments. Southern California Jews quickly took an assertive stance and formed their own active social group, called the Concordia Club. All the prominent members of the Jewish community—men and women—belonged.

The Concordia was predominantly recreational, and, therefore, was not in competition with B'nai B'rith, the national social services and networking organization established in 1843, which had become the most important and respected "voice" of the growing Jewish community. Unlike the Concordia, B'nai B'rith membership was restricted to men, many of whom were quite well-to-do.

The founders of Congregation Sinai were not doctors, lawyers, or landed gentry; by and large, they were scrappy businessmen—immigrant entrepreneurs with varying degrees of formal education who shrewdly started a garden variety of sufficiently successful businesses that allowed them to marry, start, and support young families.

With the world rapidly changing all around them, these men simply wanted a place to pray in a way that reflected their beliefs. In fact, the founders were not especially religious, although they valued communal prayer. They sought to conduct services that included more ritual observance than in the German Reform movement, but with fewer restrictions than in traditional Orthodoxy.

Los Angeles Jews had come a long way from the Sinai desert by the time they formally established Congregation Sinai in December, 1906. (The name was formally changed to Sinai Temple on June 6, 1957.) True to its time, the men took responsibility for all decisions related to worship. Women created a Jewish atmosphere in the home and took it upon themselves to promote, support, and defend social causes and cultural enrichment.

Today, Sinai is the longest surviving Conservative congregation on the West Coast, although, contrary to Sinai Temple lore, it was not the first. According to an 1894 issue of *American Israelite*, the Moses

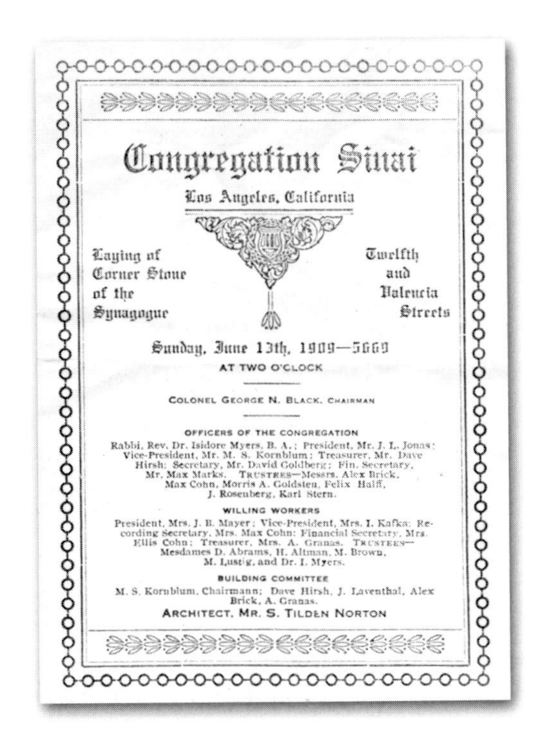

Congregation Sinai

Los Angeles, California

Laying of Corner Stone of the Synagogue

Twelfth and Valencia Streets

Sunday, June 13th, 1909—5669

AT TWO O'CLOCK

COLONEL GEORGE N. BLACK, CHAIRMAN

OFFICERS OF THE CONGREGATION

Rabbi, Rev. Dr. Isidore Myers, B. A.; President, Mr. J. L. Jonas; Vice-President, Mr. M. S. Kornblum; Treasurer, Mr. Dave Hirsh; Secretary, Mr. David Goldberg; Fin. Secretary, Mr. Max Marks. TRUSTEES—Messrs. Alex Brick, Max Cohn, Morris A. Goldsten, Felix Halff, J. Rosenberg, Karl Stern.

WILLING WORKERS

President, Mrs. J. B. Mayer; Vice-President, Mrs. I. Kafka; Recording Secretary, Mrs. Max Cohn; Financial Secretary, Mrs. Ellis Cohn; Treasurer, Mrs. A. Granas. TRUSTEES—Mesdames D. Abrams, H. Altman, M. Brown, M. Lustig, and Dr. I. Myers.

BUILDING COMMITTEE

M. S. Kornblum, Chairmann; Dave Hirsh, J. Laventhal, Alex Brick, A. Granas.

ARCHITECT, MR. S. TILDEN NORTON

Invitation to the laying of the cornerstone, June 13, 1909

Montefiore Congregation formed in 1890. It was essentially (although not officially) Conservative, conducted services in Hebrew and English, used an organ, and engaged a female choir. Following that, The People's Synagogue Beth El was created in Los Angeles on December 1, 1899, and it did identify itself as Conservative.

Sinai's First Rabbi: Isidore Myers

Rabbi Isidore Myers was the first heart and soul of Congregation Sinai. Born on February 15, 1856, in Suvalki, Poland, he received his early education at yeshiva. At age 14, he emigrated with his family to Australia, where he was educated at King's College of Melbourne University. Among his achievements, the future rabbi was an expert gymnast! Records also indicate the rabbi was proficient in eight languages: Greek, Latin, German, French, Sanskrit, Aramaic, Hebrew, and English.

We do not know where he received his *smicha* (official rabbinic authorization), but he took his first job as a rabbi at East Melbourne Hebrew Congregation, serving from 1885 to 1890. The young rabbi quickly established a reputation as an excellent writer, essayist, and scholar; he also was an accomplished poet.

From Melbourne, he went to Great Britain for five years, where he lectured extensively to promote Zionism, which was locally unpopular. Although the British differed about the need for a Jewish homeland, most agreed that Myers was a rising rabbinic star. A Canadian congregation invited him to lead it in 1895. He did, but by 1897, a congregation in San Francisco induced him to move yet again. In 1905, the Orthodox congregation Beth Israel of Los Angeles enticed the rabbi farther south.

Nearly 50 years old by then, Rabbi Myers had achieved prominence as a

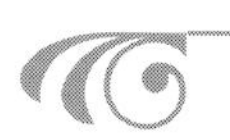

brilliant, witty, clever, and *very* independent-minded theologian. Within about a year of his arrival at Beth Israel, a group of disgruntled congregants there wanted to advance Judaism beyond the traditional style associated with Eastern Europe. They felt safe asking Rabbi Myers to conduct separate High Holiday services for them.

He agreed; but other Beth Israel congregants probably viewed this as "mutiny," and Rabbi Myers officially resigned from the congregation on July 27, 1906. He conducted High Holiday services for the "breakaway group" at Simpson Auditorium at 734 South Hope Street, with *chazzan* Marcel Katz and an all-male choir.

On December 7, 1906, the new—and newly Conservative—Congregation Sinai held its first official service at a B'nai B'rith hall located at 521 West Pico Boulevard near Figueroa Street. According to Dr. Louis G. Reynolds, Rabbi Myers was "a fine Talmudic scholar, an accomplished Hebraist, a master of the finest English and other secular literature, a keen wit and humorist. He combined all the elements which made him a most interesting lecturer, sermonizer, and teacher."

Slowly, membership grew. Convinced their congregation was viable, everyone worked hard to save, raise, and borrow enough money to purchase property at 1153 Valencia Street, where they could build a proper sanctuary of their own. On December 29, 1908, while still using the B'nai B'rith hall, Congregation Sinai incorporated in the state of California.

Rabbi and Mrs. Anna (nee Jacobson) Myers had a pretty daughter, Carmel, who was a promising young starlet in the fledgling Hollywood film industry. The Myerses also had a son in the entertainment business. Louis M. Fisch, who researched the rabbi for a 1983 article, reported that Rabbi Myers was "fond of saying he had three mountains: Mount Carmel (his daughter); Mount Zion (his son, Zion Myers, a well-known film producer); and Mount Sinai (his synagogue)."

12th and Valencia: The First House of Worship

On June 13, 1909, the cornerstone was laid for the new temple at what would forever after be referred to as "12th and Valencia." A letter of appeal for financial aid went out to all Sinai members, urging them to contribute funds to help finish construction of the new sanctuary by September—in time for the High Holidays.

On September 5, 1909, Congregation Sinai formally dedicated its first house

Temple Sinai (at time of photo Welsh Presbyterian Church)

of worship. It was designed by architect Samuel Tilden Norton, a native-born Angeleno. His mother, Berta (Greenbaum) Norton, was the first Jewish girl born in Los Angeles, and his father, Isaac, was one of the founders of the Metropolitan Building and Loan Association and, also, the Free Loan Society.

The Temple's Architecture and Design

The temple was built in a classic Greek Revival style, and had a vibrant red brick exterior—donated in entirety by the Max Marks family—that reportedly cost a total of $35,000, according to the *B'nai B'rith*

Messenger. The synagogue was a splendid and showy addition to the otherwise modest neighborhood.

The magnificent and expensive detail was evident everywhere and can still be seen today. The foyer floor was inlaid in small green and white mosaic tiles, designed in squares accented by alternating small green-, white-, and copper-colored floral patterns. The main entry chandelier was heavy brass with opaque opal glass, finished with a pineapple finial, a recognized symbol of welcome and friendship.

Mr. Norton designed the front wall of the foyer (which was the back wall of the sanctuary) on a slight curve away from the front doors, giving the foyer an expansive feel that subtly enticed visitors to enter the main sanctuary.

With two stories, including a choir loft and organ balcony above the *bimah* and a rear balcony for additional seating, the sanctuary was a large, light-filled space with six dark, carved wood gables running across an arched ceiling. In the center of the sanctuary, suspended from the ceiling, which was decorated in plaster with a Star of David surrounded by grape leaves, hung an enormous four-tiered chandelier that resembled a bronze birdcage with dangling round light bulbs. This heavy light fixture could be raised and lowered to easily change the bulbs.

No less remarkable were seven beautiful stained glass windows that decorated each side of the sanctuary, with the central windows commanding full attention. Matching Stars of David made of dark stained wood were embedded in golden glass and augmented with green, crimson, royal purple, and aqua floral styling typical of the era.

The main window at the front of the temple (which was visible inside at the rear of the balcony) was an enormous, complicated rosette design with alternating flowers and willow branches in rich, coffee-colored brown vases. True to life, the flower stems were a lush green; the petals, vibrant coral; the curly willow stems, hues of green and gold. The background of the individual panes comprising the rosette was turquoise, and lovely scrolls embellished everything.

The rosette's centerpiece was a circular pane of alternating blue-green and brown geometric segments, which harmonized all the separate design elements while allowing the flowers to visually "pop" along the periphery. The quality of this stained glass remains unmatched today and many of the colors can no longer be duplicated.

The rest of the building was compact, but functional. By the standards of today's Sinai Temple, it seems positively quaint and small. The building featured two sets of stairs: one leading to the balcony from the entrance foyer; the other, located behind the front of the sanctuary, providing access to the offices, classrooms, choir loft, and pipe organ.

The organ was situated in the choir loft above the main pulpit. Architecturally, it was framed by an enormous decorative arch gilded with a cloverleaf pattern similar to one found on most of the sanctuary's windows. A strand of tiny blue pin lights rimmed the arch's edge. Modern as these pin lights seem, unverified stories circulate that they were always there, intended to be reminiscent of the blue threads in *tsitsit* fringes.

Completing the description of the temple's physical structure, Congregation Sinai had two small kitchens since the Conservative members observed laws of *Kashruth*. One was on the first floor; the other, on the second. A resident tour guide helpfully suggested that one kitchen used to be for carbohydrates and the other, for savories!

Twelfth and Valencia must have been gorgeous when it opened, and it is well worth the trip downtown to view the artistic merit of the windows and the beauty of the original sanctuary. Still in use today by the Welsh Presbyterian Church—which purchased it in 1924 and let Sinai continue to use it for nearly two more years—the building received historical landmark status on April 20, 1977. It remains open to the public during the Welsh congregation's Sunday morning worship hour, as well as during earlier Sunday morning services conducted there by a Hispanic outreach congregation that ministers, Revival style, in Spanish, to a packed house.

The Welsh church (with a donation from Sinai Temple) has spent significant funds to retrofit the building for earthquake safety and to partially restore and preserve the sanctuary, but, sadly, that congregation is, itself, on the verge of extinction as a result of the natural aging of its congregants and their westward migration away from downtown.

The Temple's Music and the Organ

It is vital to understand the importance of music—and specifically, the pipe organ—not only to the development of the original Congregation Sinai, but also to the character and definition of Sinai Temple throughout its history.

Jews have always uttered the same prayers in Hebrew, whether they come from Topeka, Toulouse, or Tehran. But for conversation, most of Sinai's original members spoke English as a second language. Over a dozen languages may have been spoken during Sinai's first years, making communication a real challenge.

Everyone worked hard to learn the language of their adopted country, and Rabbi Myers conducted services in Hebrew and English. Other local congregations, in deference to their primarily European constituency, conducted their services in Hebrew and Yiddish.

Music, though, has always transcended spoken language, binding people together spiritually from the beginning of time. Rabbi Myers and Sinai's founders understood this. The Sinai service, replete with beautiful melodies, helped bring

Choir loft and organ balcony

Sanctuary with rear balcony for extra seating

people in, made them feel comfortable, and gave them a sense of belonging.

Marcel Katz was the temple's first cantor. Archival documents provide almost no information about him except to say that he had a magnificent voice. (Unfortunately, he left the following year and records do not indicate why.) Sinai, similar to many congregations then, engaged a choir to augment the cantor. But the pipe organ was a serious departure for a Jewish congregation in 1909.

It required effort to play, which contradicted traditional prohibitions against work on Shabbat. All the same, it was impressive in sight and sound, and its extravagance reflected the upward mobility of hardworking immigrants who were proud to be able to (barely) afford it. Historian Dr. Max Vorspan indicates in

his seminal book *History of the Jews of Los Angeles* that the organ played when the temple first opened.

Spanning the length of the entire balcony above the *bimah,* and crafted by the renowned Los Angeles–based organ maker Murray Harris Co., the organ's individual pipes, painstakingly hand-painted with golden leaves—a testament to the skilled artisans of bygone days—are still in excellent working order. You can hear this instrument played weekly during the Sunday Welsh Presbyterian service, and, since the church is no longer full of parishioners, the organ sounds especially grand as its music reverberates through the sanctuary. Listening to hymns sung in Welsh, one gets a sense of what immigrants might have experienced, not knowing the words to the songs, but having a clear sense of their holiness.

To this day, Sinai Temple in Los Angeles is synonymous with organ music. Cantor Moses Alter joined the temple after Cantor Katz in either 1907 or 1909; records are unclear. Many famous cantors and *chazzanim* have graced the congregation with their voices. Several have composed music that has since become famous within the Jewish liturgical music canon.

Ritual at Sinai: Then and Now

Congregation Sinai (and later, Sinai Temple) has always been blessed with a wonderful *shammes*. A *shammes*, or ritual director, is responsible for the implementation of Jewish ritual in and around the synagogue.

The synagogue's first order of business has always been its daily morning prayer service, with *Mincha-Ma'ariv* davened toward day's end. Both services include the recitation of the Mourner's *Kaddish,* a prayer that cannot be said without the presence of a *minyan* (ten adult worshippers). Traditionally limited to men, Sinai Temple's ritual committee officially acknowledged women's prayer as acceptable for making a full *minyan* in the 1990s.

Sinai has always had dependable morning and afternoon *minyanim*. It is one of the most important functions of a Conservative synagogue, not only for its members, but also as a service to the Jewish community at large. For those who have lost a loved one or are observing a *yahrzeit,* the recitation of the Mourner's *Kaddish* is a *mitzvah*. It is an affirmation of life and of faith in God—especially important during times of emotional transition—and its recitation within a group can provide great comfort.

Rabbis on the Move

Rabbi Myers stayed with Sinai, helping it grow until 1912, when he left. No conclusive evidence exists to explain why such a highly esteemed leader should move on,

Rudolph Farber, Rabbi 1912–1915

but *History of the Jews of Los Angeles* indicates that he subsequently attempted to form another, new "People's" congregation locally.

The temple brought in Rabbi Rudolph Farber, a highly respected rabbi who received his training in Europe and his rabbinic authorization from Professors Kaempf and Stein of Prague. Prior to joining Sinai, he held positions in Des Moines, Texarkana (Arkansas), Detroit, Chicago, and Seattle. Records indicate his first wife (whose name is not mentioned) died during the birth of their second child. His second wife was Etta Crocker, and they had three children together.

Little more is known about Rabbi Farber's Sinai sojourn except that he served the temple for only three years due to increasingly poor health. In 1915, shortly after World War I began in Europe, but before the United States committed troops to action overseas, he left. Congregation Sinai set about regaining its equilibrium, as the entire world around it changed.

Stained glass window, exterior view, 12th and Valencia

Chapter Two

Revolving Rabbis

War is the quintessential metaphor for transition—change in leadership; change of nationality; change in what we do, with whom, when, and where. How we adapt to change determines how well we will survive. War also reminds us how to count. We count the days. We count the number of lives lost. We count our blessings. And we count our blessings again.

No one dreamed that the war, the Great War, the first truly international, geopolitical conflict, would be but a precursor to a second, 25 years later. People wrongly believed that no one would ever wage war again with the stakes so high.

In 1917, the United States entered World War I, long after most other countries. Sinai was already two years into new leadership under

Rabbi David Liknaitz, about whom there is almost no information, except that he worked with Cantor Jacob Weinstock, who also began in 1915. Among the immigrants who comprised Sinai's membership, the war seemed to foster a sense of patriotism, as well as gratitude for being able to live freely in America.

A mandatory draft conscripted all eligible young men, and many men outside the draft age also volunteered. Almost every family in the country had a member or close relative enlisted. Congregation Sinai was no different. Of course, not everyone came home. Each fatality affected the entire close-knit community.

As the personal losses mounted, the congregation collectively endured one more: the departure of Rabbi Liknaitz, their third rabbi, again leaving after only three years.

The Arrival of Rabbi Moses Rosenthal

Rabbi Moses Rosenthal came from New York to replace Rabbi Liknaitz at the High Holidays in 1918. He was 31 years old when he arrived with his wife and their 11-month-old daughter. A large delegation of congregants met the family at Santa Fe Station. The rabbi was strictly observant, so one must wonder what would make him travel across the country for a new job with an avowed Conservative congregation.

Born in New York City in 1887, he studied at Yeshiva Eitz Chaim, which became known as the Rabbinical College. He then attended the College of the City of New York, graduating with a bachelor's degree in 1910, followed by scholarship at the Jewish Theological Seminary of America. His wife, a graduate of the New York City School of Expression, taught and gave public recitals.

Moses Rosenthal was ordained in 1914. His first job was as leader of a congregation in New York City's Washington Heights neighborhood. He held the position for five years, during which he helped it grow in membership and inspired its congregants to significantly fill its coffers. He was a well-respected community organizer with ties to Zionist groups, youth groups, and the International Hatikva Collegiate movement. Rabbi Rosenthal was also a founder of the Washington Heights YMHA.

His main passion, however, was the Young Israel movement, which he founded with Professor Israel Friedlaender, and which was a rapidly growing national organization resolved to "make and keep young men true to Judaism." Like Sinai's first rabbi, Rabbi Rosenthal was committed to Zionism and had a very strong social conscience. He worked hard to impart a sense of moral obligation and responsibility to his new flock. Upon joining Congregation Sinai, the rabbi started a new chapter of Young Israel called "The Willing Workers," which was very active under his leadership.

With the war in full swing when he arrived, the rabbi made it a point to welcome soldiers and sailors to all services, year-round. One of them, Bernard Elman, was so impressed with Sinai that he assigned $1,000 of his insurance policy to the congregation in the event he was killed. To the best of the rabbi's knowledge as of the next year, the young man was safe and scheduled to return to Los Angeles.

Rabbi Rosenthal was an outspoken and passionate patriot. Every week, he would preach from the *bimah* about the war, explaining the current political situation as he saw it. He felt it was an obligation of the congregation to support the war effort and to understand what was happening and why. Moreover, he regularly reminded the congregation that returning veterans had seen things too horrible to imagine, that they could not help but be changed by their traumatic experiences. To expect them to return to "normal"—the way life used to be—was unrealistic. They would need time, and help, to readjust to civilian life, and congregants were encouraged to warmly welcome Jewish veterans returning to the community.

One of the phenomena of war is an increase in the number of marriages hastily arranged before servicemen's deployment; another, sadly, is an increase in funerals. Congregation Sinai published in its 1918–1919 Annual Review a list of its war dead: 54 men. As this is the only document of its kind in the archives, it is unclear whether those names represented the casualties in that year alone—the United States only sent over its first troops in June of 1917—or whether the list was comprehensive for the war's duration and included names from the previous six months, too. Either way, Rabbi Rosenthal frequently acknowledged in his writings and sermons what a tremendously painful year it had been for the parishioners at 12th and Valencia.

A Rabbi's Role Then and Now

It is interesting to compare the role of Rabbi Rosenthal to the role of rabbis today at Sinai Temple. Ninety years ago, many of the congregants probably didn't read English; foreign language papers were scarce, if they existed at all. The

synagogue was probably the best place, and the rabbi the most educated and trustworthy person, for most members to learn about international news.

Today's congregation is highly educated and many members are extremely sophisticated. With access to numerous news sources in a variety of languages, people no longer depend on the rabbi as the "definitive" authority for disseminating information or interpreting it, although the rabbi's opinion about issues of key moral or political concern is still quite important and sought after. Sinai's rabbis strive to present all sides of a situation and to avoid public endorsement of any one particular viewpoint.

Reverend Cantor Silverman, Cantor 1918–1940

Good News on the Home Front: The Reverend Cantor Abraham Silverman

An important part of Rabbi Rosenthal's legacy was hiring a new cantor named Abraham Silverman, son of the famous Cantor Wolf Silverman, and grandfather of current Sinai member Diane Silverman Miller. (Records do not indicate why Cantor Weinstock left or where he may have gone.)

Abraham Silverman, born in 1887 in Russia, came to Los Angeles with his wife and three children via

Brooklyn, New York, and commenced his loyal 22 years of service to Congregation Sinai on Thursday, December 5, 1918, the eighth day of Chanukah.

His arrival truly was cause for celebration. It marked the end of a compulsory 2-month ban on all public gatherings—including religious worship—to help prevent further spread of a deadly and raging influenza pandemic. Known as "Spanish Flu" or *La Grippe*, the influenza of 1918–1919 was a global disaster. Families feared death not only from war, but from disease, as well. And with good reason: more people died of influenza in that single year than in four years of the Black Death during the Middle Ages. Nearly half of the American soldiers who died, died not of war injuries but of the flu.

The new cantor, a magnificent baritone, included in his repertoire many of the songs his father had composed and which were chanted throughout the most famous *shuls* of Europe. At Sinai, a well-trained Jewish choir accompanied him. This was something new; until then not all choir members had been Jewish. Rabbi Rosenthal felt strongly that Jews best captured the appropriate soulfulness so essential to Jewish synagogue music. In his own words, "The Jewish choir has supplied ... that peculiar feeling which goes straight to the suffering heart of the Jew." Cantor Silverman assented to the rabbi's wish. Congregation Sinai approved its new choir and loved Cantor Silverman so much that in a musical program written long after he passed away, he was described as having "walked with angels."

The ability to congregate once again in public, plus the beauty of Cantor Silverman's voice, brought increasing numbers of worshippers to Friday night services (which were better attended than the Shabbat morning service), and it became apparent that increased seating capacity would soon be needed. Thus began the campaign to create a "Greater Sinai," which would not only include more seats for more members, but also give the synagogue a greater role in the community at large.

Envisioning a "Greater Sinai"

By 1919, Congregation Sinai had been the premier Conservative congregation on the West Coast of the United States for a decade. Affiliation with United Synagogue of America gave it solid standing at a national level and spoke to the congregation's commitment to uphold and perpetuate the tenets of Conservative Judaism. In fact, records indicate that the rabbi refused to officiate at two intermarriages that year.

Sinai could proudly boast a beautiful sanctuary, growing membership, Sunday school, and a daily school, too. Still, the rabbi and congregation envisioned more. "Greater Sinai" referred to a plan to enlarge the schoolhouse and operate a "Sinai Hebrew Academy." According to Rabbi Rosenthal, its aim was to "prove the entire compatibility of Judaism and Americanism, from which the Jewish spirit shall radiate, ministering to the religious, cultural, civic, social, and physical welfare of the Jewish community and the Jewish people—namely, a House of Prayer, a House of Study and Education, a House of Assembly or Social Service and Recreation."

Thirty-one men worked as a building committee and helped secure, in a matter of three weeks, pledges amounting to $40,000 toward an overall goal of $100,000. In 1920!

The 1920s "Roar" to Life

It was not an easy time to maintain traditional Jewish standards in a secular society. The Flapper Era had begun—a wild time in a young country exuberant from its recent military victory. In an effort to curb the consumption of liquor and impose strict moral standards, Congress, in 1920, enacted legislation that came to be known as Prohibition.

The decade was called the "Roaring Twenties" for good reason. Men returned from war with battle scars, yet full of bravado; bootlegged whiskey was illicitly imbibed in backroom speakeasies. Traditional modesty in women gave way to emancipation and, eventually, hard-won women's suffrage. Young ladies bobbed their hair, hemlines went up, defenses went down, and cigarette smoking became the rage among fashionable women.

And yet, there was balance in Los Angeles's Jewish community between having fun and doing good. The creation of Hillcrest Country Club, established by a dynamic group of people for social enjoyment, represented only one aspect of the community's interests. At the same time, they also established the Bikkur Cholim Society, which later became Mt. Sinai Hospital and then, eventually, today's Cedars-Sinai Medical Center. An old-age home was opened; numerous societies formed to cater to the needs of the various immigrant Jewish communities; and war relief campaigns continued. These were but a few of the activities of the day.

It is really quite a statement about the constancy of Judaism, the commitment to *tikkun olam*, and, even more, the remarkable character of Congregation Sinai, that during a decade known for its decadence, the temple not only retained its members, but actually grew to such extent that the synagogue could no longer accommodate all the members with their extended families, friends, and nonmembers who wanted to attend High Holiday services.

Then, as even now, seating played an important role at Congregation Sinai. In order to raise funds, members were offered the option of purchasing "lifetime" seats in the location of their choice, for a large contribution in addition to the annual dues. The more one contributed, the "better" the seat one could have, even retaining it in perpetuity for the High Holidays.

The influx of new members at Congregation Sinai in the early 1920s was due partly to the growing Jewish community in Los Angeles, partly to the increasing popularity of Conservative Judaism in America, and partly to a change in clergy, yet again.

In 1922, Rabbi Rosenthal left. It is possible that the minutes of the board of directors indicate the reason, but the original and only copy is nearly impossible to read with its highly ornate penmanship fading on fragile paper. Suffice it to say that in 1922, a mere four years after joining Congregation Sinai, the fourth rabbi exited and the temple engaged its fifth leader, Rabbi Mayer Winkler.

Fourth and New Hampshire

Chapter Three

The Rabbi Winkler Years

Rabbi Eliyahu Mayer Winkler was born in Hungary in 1882. He received his *smicha* and a doctoral degree at the same time from Israelitsch-Theologische Lehranstalt in Wien (Vienna) around 1912 or 1913. His certification was very special because it authorized him to act as a judge and attorney for the Jewish community that, as a group, eschewed the secular courts. He married his wife, Gizella, in 1907 and they had three children before leaving Hungary: Irvin, Nelly, and Rudolf. Little is known about his early career, but by the 1920s, Rabbi Winkler—often referred to as Dr. Winkler—was one of the rabbis at the Dohány Synagogue (also called the Great Synagogue) in the heart of Budapest. Beautifully restored in the 1990s, that synagogue seats 3,000 worshippers and is still in use.

Rabbi Mayer Winkler and Family

The Great Expansion at Sinai

Rabbi Winkler did well in Pennsylvania and attracted the attention of Dr. Louis G. Reynolds, a prominent member of Congregation Sinai, who paid him a visit at the *shul*. He and the board knew Sinai would be needing a new rabbi in the near future, although it is not clear whether the presiding Rabbi Rosenthal knew it yet himself. Dr. Reynolds invited Rabbi Winkler to Los Angeles to meet Sinai's board of directors.

As was true in much of Eastern Europe then, the political climate in Hungary became hostile toward Jews. By 1920, Rabbi Winkler recognized the threat to his family, as well as to the greater Jewish community, so he left with his brood for America.

Rodeph Shalom Congregation, in Homestead, Pennsylvania, near Pittsburgh, welcomed him as their senior rabbi. The entire congregation truly took him to its heart. A natural linguist (the rabbi already spoke Hungarian, Yiddish, German, and Hebrew), he quickly learned English and soon became very active in the war relief effort, the YMHA, and many other Jewish communal endeavors.

Impressed, they immediately offered him a 1-year contract (and, one may conclude, they informed Rabbi Rosenthal of his termination). Rabbi Winkler accepted and packed up his family again to head west. He was about 40 years old.

From all accounts, Congregation Sinai and its new rabbi were thrilled with one another. The hallmark of Rabbi Winkler's mission at Sinai might best be described in one word: communication. Good communication was the foundation for learning, teaching, and—he hoped—growth. One of the first things he did was to write a monthly newsletter detailing everything happening at Sinai. First distributed in February 1923, it was originally entitled *Sinai's Call*. Nearly 85 years later, a similar monthly mailer still goes out and is called *Sinai Speaks*.

The act of speaking itself furthered Rabbi Winkler's career. A born communicator, and highly charismatic, he soon created an impressive niche for himself in the new field of radio broadcasting. He delivered a short weekly program on Sundays on station KHJ that included a sermon and topical issues. It was called (or later came to be called) *Synagogue of the Air*, and was aimed at a general audience of both Jews and gentiles. For temple members who couldn't come to *shul* on Shabbat, it was a wonderful way to hear a *d'var Torah*. For non-Jews, it provided excellent interfaith public relations. And for unaffiliated Jews, it provided a weekly "advertisement" for the temple, which produced a terrific ancillary benefit: Sinai membership grew.

New members also meant more children. The rabbi placed great emphasis on communicating with Sinai's children, as well as connecting with their parents and other adults via newsletter and radio. He yearned to make the religious school the best in the West. While it already had a healthy enrollment, Rabbi Winkler wanted to see it increase, and he also wanted to expand the scope of what children learned.

Rabbi Winkler's predecessor, Rabbi Rosenthal, first envisioned this expansion as "Greater Sinai." It would encompass a new building with state-of-the-art educational facilities, meeting halls, banquet rooms, and more—everything necessary to make Congregation Sinai the nexus of Jewish communal life. Membership already embraced Rabbi Rosenthal's concept and Rabbi Winkler successfully moved it forward by pushing fundraising initiatives at all levels of the congregation.

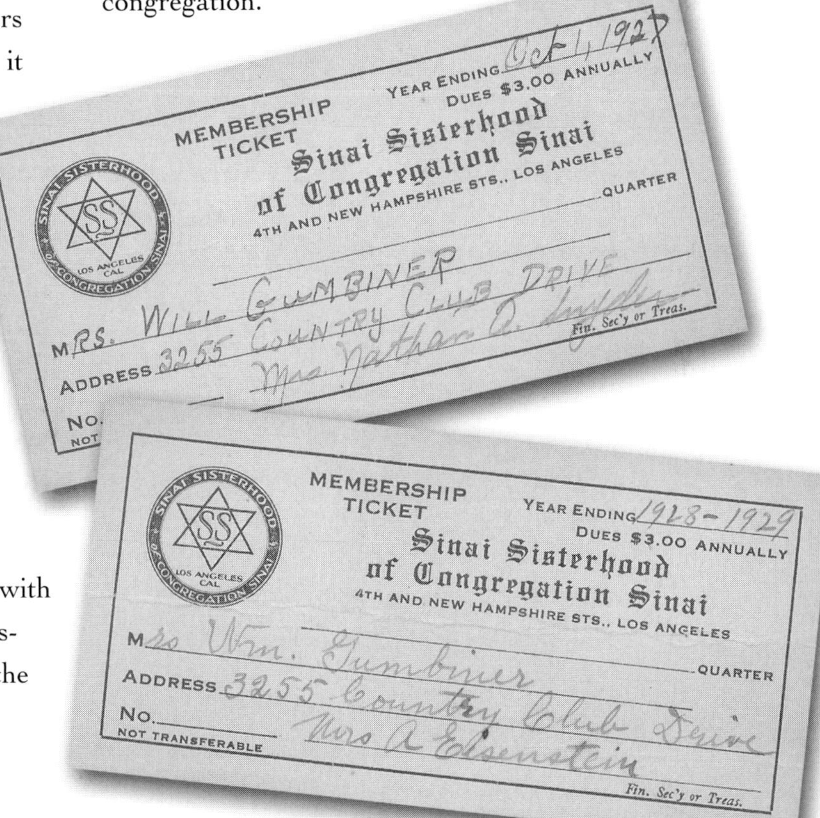

MEMBERSHIP TICKET
YEAR ENDING Oct 1, 1927
DUES $3.00 ANNUALLY
Sinai Sisterhood of Congregation Sinai
4TH AND NEW HAMPSHIRE STS., LOS ANGELES
QUARTER
MRS. Will Gumbiner
ADDRESS 3255 Country Club Drive
Mrs. Nathan A. Snyder
Fin. Sec'y or Treas.
NO.
NOT

MEMBERSHIP TICKET
YEAR ENDING 1928-1929
DUES $3.00 ANNUALLY
Sinai Sisterhood of Congregation Sinai
4TH AND NEW HAMPSHIRE STS., LOS ANGELES
M.rs Wm. Gumbiner
QUARTER
ADDRESS 3255 Country Club Drive
NO.
NOT TRANSFERABLE
Mrs A Eisenstein
Fin. Sec'y or Treas.

Membership tickets

SINAI'S CALL

Volume 1 Number 1
Adar 5883 February 1923

LOYALTY TO SINAI
By Rabbi Mayer Winkler

I take the pleasure of introducing this Bulletin to the members and friends of my Congregation for the purpose of bringing the message of Sinai to every faithful follower of traditional Judaism. At the threshold of a new period of a spiritual revival in our midst, it is necessary for every one of us, young and old, to be loyal to the cause which Sinai exemplifies. Standing on the holy ground of Tradition, we are striving to bring our young people back into the knowledge of our glorious history, of our wonderful literature and the sublime ideals of our Bible. Let us unite so that we can stand together and create the means by which our holy task can be carried out successfully. Let us build a new Synagogue for worship and a Center for social activities so that our work may expand and grow. Let us be inspired by the spirit of love, of self-sacrifice and loyalty to Sinai. Let us establish a sanctuary where our young people may drink of the living waters of the eternal truths of Sinai.

The temple planned for its physical expansion using the adjacent lot it already owned. Plans were drawn up by the architectural firm of Edelman and Barnett Architects for Sinai Hebrew Academy, a three-story plus basement structure in the residence-style of design. It was to be a two-tone brick and complementary colored cast-stone building that would include, among other things, a formal library, administrative offices, classrooms, a modern gymnasium (68 by 49 feet), a kitchen, two assembly rooms seating 200 and 600, and a stage, all to be equipped with the best plumbing, heating, ventilation, and electricity.

But by the beginning of 1923, the elders of the congregation realized several things: first, the main sanctuary at 12th and Valencia would soon be too small. Sure enough, by the High Holidays that year, the entire membership could no longer fit into the space, so the temple rented the Philharmonic Auditorium for services. Second, and maybe even more important, the Jewish population of Los Angeles had started leaving downtown, moving west. The Boyle Heights neighborhood would soon lose its luster and with it, its vibrancy, which, in turn, could threaten the temple's survival.

Therefore, the plan—grand as it was—had to be scrapped. Faced with changing specifications and shifting demographics, the board decided it had to sell the old, yet still dearly loved, property and purchase a new site for building in a more suitable neighborhood. Based on real estate trends, everyone agreed the best area would be what is now called Koreatown. According to board minutes, the original lot that Congregation Sinai purchased—on February 14, 1923—was located at 3rd and New Hampshire, but the temple was ultimately built on the opposite corner at 4th and New Hampshire.

Rabbi Winkler's first year as spiritual leader passed, and both he and Congregation Sinai were extremely pleased with one another. When the board prepared in February 1924 to renew his contract, its by-laws only permitted a maximum employment period of two years. To give their leader a resounding vote of confidence, the board amended the by-laws and gave him a 5-year agreement.

The dynamic Rabbi Winkler dedicated himself to bringing honor and glory to Congregation Sinai, and Sinai's growth mirrored that of Los Angeles itself. At the end of 1924, temple membership stood at 389 families. Families that came to the United States 20 years earlier and worked as laborers in the garment industry now owned clothing factories themselves. Doctors, lawyers, and other professionals also made up the Jewish population of the city.

Between 1924 and 1929, the United States experienced tremendous growth all around. The movie business, soon to become the symbol of Los Angeles, expanded with the birth of Metro-Goldwyn-Mayer Studio. Mr. Mayer often made screenings possible for the temple. Silent motion pictures gave way to "talkies" with the 1927 debut of *The Jazz Singer*. Despite Prohibition (or maybe even because of it), the times seemed intoxicating ... nothing seemed impossible.

During this same period, IBM began its long run of technological dominance, first within the United States and, later, internationally. Philo T. Farnsworth introduced an invention that would one day become television. Werner Heisenberg explained quantum mechanics. Birth control received the endorsement of the American Medical Association. And Germany's post–WWI debt was restructured, which, at least temporarily, gave the rest of the world a little breathing room.

Fourth and New Hampshire

In 1925, in Iran, Reza Khan ascended the throne to establish the Pahlevi dynasty. He modernized Iran's infrastructure, Moslem law, and dress codes for women. In 1926, in London, the future Queen Elizabeth II was born.

Building for the Future

During this time of peace and prosperity Congregation Sinai's board of directors decided to press forward. After purchasing the property at 4th and New Hampshire,

Memorial tablets

the board voted to interview several architects, and had initial meetings with a few.

For its new home, Sinai wanted something grand—majestic, soaring, spectacular—something that would reflect the vaunted position that Sinai held in the Los Angeles community and the larger community of Conservative Jewish congregations in America. The very language used by a temple says much about the congregation.

Almost everything ever written for or about Congregation Sinai, regardless of the subject, used superlatives. Everything was always the biggest, the best, grandest, most glorious. Sinai, in its own opinion, was worthy of, and entitled to, the most famous, most well-known, best regarded ... everything.

While some of the extravagant language can be attributed to the more formal writing style of nearly 100 years ago, much of it reflected the distinct attitude of the congregation—an attitude that persists, to some degree, to this day. "Good" alone was never enough when it came to Sinai. Everyone hired and everything purchased had to bring prestige not just competence to the congregation.

Specifications for the new temple were given to competing architectural firms, and Sinai eventually chose S. Tilden Norton and Frederick Wallis. Norton was the same architect who built Sinai's first synagogue at 12th and Valencia. The firm's fee, 5 percent of the building cost, was standard at the time, but for no additional fee, the board further convinced Norton to supervise all the construction. All board members except one favored this proposal.

To help pay for the cost of the new building, Sinai sold the old one. The Welsh Presbyterian Church bought the building for $50,000, making a down payment of $25,000 in cash, and agreed to allow the Sinai congregation to use the building, at minimal rent, for the next year, or until the new temple was completed.

All the activities typically associated with building a new synagogue took place. But fundraising caused the greatest concern, even more than usual, because many people who had pledged money either reneged on their obligations or were extremely slow in paying. The board worked hard to address the growing discrepancy between anticipated costs and available cash. Several intrepid board members in succession took on the task of trying to secure promised funds from congregants, but their failure led each, in turn, to resign in frustration and with regret. One stalwart, Benjamin Platt, who also served for over 20 years as Sinai's president, dipped into his own wallet several times—to the tune of over $50,000—to forestall delays to the building's progress.

That was a *tremendous* amount of money back then, and readers might assume, wrongly, that Mr. Platt was an extremely wealthy man. While it is true that he owned a successful music business that many years later became quite lucrative,

Groundbreaking, February 15, 1925. From left to right: Eugene Rosen, A. Klugman, William Feuer, Emil Brown, Benjamin Platt, Rabbi Winkler, Dr. L. G. Reynolds, Abe Lutz, Moses Tannenbaum, and S. Sagal.

According to Temple B'nai B'rith's Rabbi Edgar F. Magnin, a distinguished guest at the inaugural ceremonies, "Every brick represents a heart throb. And the cement that binds these bricks together is symbolic of the unity and harmony that exist in the congregation."

his contributions to Congregation Sinai—both in terms of time invested and money donated—have been remembered and characterized recently by a most highly regarded rabbi in Los Angeles as a true and earnest measure of his devotion to God, Judaism, and the temple. (He also made sure members of the board signed personal notes to guarantee his repayment.)

Ultimately, many different bank loans were secured through the clever and experienced business acumen of Ben Platt and a select group of board members. The cornerstone was laid on April 12, 1925; approximately 700–800 people attended. Judge Isaac Pacht, an attorney and board member, who had carefully negotiated all of the contracts related to the new building, received the honor of being asked to deliver the dedicatory speech. It is reported that he spoke beautifully and with heartfelt sentiment.

Finance continued to be a problem for the congregation throughout the period of construction. As the High Holidays approached, it was decided to hold the services in the skeleton of the building to make more apparent to members the dire need for construction money. Around this time, people began to use the term "New Sinai" when referring to the *shul*, and once again, "lifetime" seats were sold to raise money. Members who already owned "lifetime" seats at 12th and Valencia were compensated with similar ones when 4th and New Hampshire opened.

Finally, in 1926, the new Congregation Sinai temple was completed, and the time came to say farewell to the still beautiful building at 12th and Valencia. A closing ceremony was scheduled; unfortunately, Cantor Silverman was unwell and unable to attend. Rabbi Winkler spoke this prayer to close the service:

> *For the sentiments we have expressed here in (this) House of Prayer, our hopes and aspirations in joy and sorrow, grant, O Lord, that we may still continue to keep thy Law and thy Traditions in the New House of Worship to be dedicated to Sinai. O Lord, I love the habitation of thy house and the place where thy glory dwelleth. The prayers of so many sorrowing and exulting hearts, the supplications of the orphaned shall not be in vain, they are embodied as the ministering angels and in their glory spread their wings of eternity upon this congregation. Bless us in our coming and in our going out.*

In an account published in the *B'nai B'rith Messenger*, "a solemn hush fell upon the congregation as the last words of the powerful prayer rang through the vaulted hall and closed with the sonorous tone of the organ."

The opening of the new temple at 4th and New Hampshire on September 5,

1926, was a joyous celebration—exactly seventeen years to the day after the first temple opened! Rabbi Winkler presided over the festivities; local and state dignitaries attended. In his remarks, Rabbi Winkler expressed the relationship he saw between Congregation Sinai's achievement and the spirit of democracy and religious freedom allowed in the United States. It was a very apt observation, especially in light of the massive waves of Jewish immigrants who had arrived in America since the end of World War I, and the rabbi's own flight from his native country just five years before.

Beauty in the Sight of God

The synagogue that S. Tilden Norton and Frederick Wallis built was glorious, indeed. Still standing and in use today by the Korean Philadelphia Presbyterian Church, it remains a beautiful house of worship, decorated with splendid, sophisticated, vibrantly colored stained glass windows of varying shapes and sizes; majestic chandeliers and light fixtures; individual seating (rather than pews); and an inspiring, light-drenched overhead circular art glass window depicting the twelve tribes of Israel.

Built into the front of the building, actually the rear of the main sanctuary, is a semicircular stained glass window designed as a giant sunburst. From the outside, the design seems interesting, although the colors appear drab, but from the inside, one sees something quite different. Every morning when the sun rises, it ascends into the window's sunbeams to "merge" with them, creating a brilliant flare of warm color that saturates the sanctuary and inspires those lucky few people who arrive early enough to see it.

The graceful and flowing design of the generously sized balcony bears striking resemblance to the curved lines of the balcony at 12th and Valencia. But seating on the main floor—dark polished wood with velvet upholstery—is much fancier and more spacious than before and almost wraps around the *bimah*.

The *bimah* is a two-tiered semicircle design with a large lower area that can accommodate a crowd, accented by a smaller upper area immediately next to the ark. When the synagogue opened, the ark featured beautiful gilded wood panels artfully created by Peter Krasnow, at that time the young, "starving artist" husband of Rose Krasnow, the rabbi's executive assistant who also ran confirmation classes. It was she who recommended her husband for the job, and his commission was significant because it was the first time Sinai hired a local Jewish artist to create original, interpretive art as an integral part of the holy sanctuary.

Dr. L. G. Reynolds, president of Congregation Sinai, wrote in the dedication program: "It is our intention that it serve not only as a House of Worship but also if not principally as a center of Jewish learning and Jewish social activity. Sinai will stand for tradition, Zionism and Hebrew culture. It is our fondest dream that the future generations raised under the aegis of this Congregation, may truthfully and honestly exclaim, 'God Cometh Out of Sinai.'"

Peter Krasnow deservedly received recognition for his contribution, and became a highly respected artist in Los Angeles. His sculptures were regularly featured in well-known art galleries and, today, are included in several important private collections. Fortunately, the ark panels became beloved and familiar symbols in the temple, and they were preserved when the congregation moved to Wilshire and Beverly Glen, where they now adorn the exterior of Kohn Chapel and "float" as the doors of the *Aron Kodesh* inside.

The new temple not only addressed the need for additional seating for the increased membership (total seating capacity around 1,300), but it also provided a large social hall that could be used for synagogue functions and *simchas* and doubled as an auditorium for the school. The school itself, which had been bursting at the seams for years, finally had adequate space for its growing student body. New and improved classrooms gave children in Sinai schools state-of-the-art facilities.

Fourth and New Hampshire became home to the very first official Congregation Sinai Library: The Moses and Hannah Tannenbaum Library, dedicated on December 10, 1939, in their memory by their children. Even today, the Korean church uses this space as a library, and it is filled to the rafters.

While some of the building's structural innovations might seem mundane by current standards, they were very smart and forward-thinking for 1925. Large classrooms had doors at each end and a folding center partition that could divide the space into two smaller spaces. Most of the rooms also had skylights, bringing in extra daylight to make the learning environment more cheerful as well as more economical in terms of electricity costs. Norton and Wallis designed a projection room above the social hall so Sinai could screen movies, and a rehearsal room behind the stage, with stage door entry and side access.

Although there was only one kitchen instead of two, it was easily eight times larger than each one at 12th and Valencia. It was located downstairs, and immediately adjacent to it was a space that was smaller than the social hall upstairs, but large enough to function as a school cafeteria, or hold a gracious *oneg Shabbat* or an informal meal. Also downstairs were the boiler rooms with their original gas-powered turbine heaters. Still in working condition, they are almost never used anymore due to the extremely high cost of fuel: they are a real tribute to mechanical engineering of the early 20th century.

Trouble in Paradise

The official minutes of the board of directors meetings from October 7, 1926, through February 13, 1929, have vanished and, along with them, our ability to corroborate anecdotal evidence about exactly what happened at the temple during the first few years in the new building. We *do* know that trouble started brewing over Rabbi Winkler.

As head of the congregation, Rabbi Winkler requested permission from the board to attend all the various department, school, youth, and adult social meetings. He said it would give him more direct and better insight into the inner workings and needs of these different areas of the temple. The board concurred. However, in time, it seems the rabbi overstepped what others thought were appropriate boundaries, and he received serious complaints from Sisterhood about his interference.

Of far greater concern to the rabbi was the growing difference of opinion between himself and the board regarding his authority to run Sinai's schools. Rabbi Winkler was very "Old World" and a traditionalist in his view of a rabbi's function: not only should he minister to the spiritual needs of his congregation, but he also had the obligation of, responsibility for, and was entitled to the privilege of, determining how the synagogue's children should be taught.

Panels on the door of the Ark by Peter Krasnow

A. M. Tonnis served as the schools' director. Students, their parents, and, especially, the board liked Mr. Tonnis. He quickly proved himself adept at administering the daily Hebrew school, the religious school, and the confirmation program, and as a trained educator, he also began to contribute his own ideas toward the curriculum. Rabbi Winkler took this as a direct challenge. From the minutes of the regular and special board meetings after 1929, it seems Mr. Tonnis and Rabbi Winkler engaged in some sort of power struggle—overt or not is unclear—but the board backed the more modern Mr. Tonnis and relieved the rabbi of his authority to run Sinai's schools.

Confirmation class with Rabbi Winkler, Cantor Silverman, and Mrs. Rose Krasnow

Lecturn on the Bimah

When Rabbi Winkler lost this privilege, he protested to the board, which acknowledged his complaint, but stood by its decision. It was the first real sign of the growing strength of the board, its willingness to exercise power over the clergy, and its tremendous influence on the direction of the congregation. It would definitely not be the last.

NUMBER 6

100.00

Congregation Sinai

Los Angeles, California, May 15 1927

For Value Received, Congregation Sinai, a religious corporation, organized and existing under and by virtue of the laws of the State of California, promises to pay to or order, the Sum of One Hundred Dollars ($100.00) in ten equal Annual Installments, commencing January 1st, 1928, together with interest at the rate of six (6) per cent per annum, payable semi-annually on the first days of May and November. Principal and interest of this note shall be payable at the office of the Congregation Sinai, in the City of Los Angeles, California.

GOLD NOTE

Congregation Sinai

BY

BY SECRETARY

Cancelled 1/31/28

Ten-Year $100 Gold Note Certificate with $3.00 interest paid by Sinai every six months. Cancelled when paid in full.

Chapter Four

It's Always About the Money

Never one to shrink from public speaking, during late 1929 and early 1930, Rabbi Winkler espoused controversial positions on several issues and made various injudicious public statements, much to the consternation of the board and congregation. In 1929, the directors finally decided to remove him from the pulpit and buy out his remaining contract. They offered an exit package worth $9,150, payable with one large sum up front, along with notes for monthly payment over the next year. According to Rabbi Winkler's son Rudolf ("Rudy"), the decision (itself considered controversial by some members) left the rabbi profoundly shocked and disappointed for the rest of his life.

Rabbi Winkler Leaves, and the Great Depression Starts

Before the rabbi resigned, members had been trickling away. But after the rabbi left, membership plummeted. It is impossible to determine any one definitive cause since the congregation had been cleft by Rabbi Winkler's presence as well as his departure. Many members who opposed the rabbi had begun to leave the congregation even before he resigned. It was the only way they knew to protest his leadership. But those members who supported and dearly loved Rabbi Winkler couldn't believe he was asked to leave, or how it was done. So they protested in the only reasonable way *they* knew possible—they also left!

In addition to those members who left to "make a statement," there were many members who had lost everything they owned in the stock market crash of 1929. They were having trouble putting food on their tables, not to mention maintaining membership in a synagogue. Many humbly asked for reductions in their annual dues from the normal family rate of $60 to $42; others simply resigned, with deep regret.

Congregation Sinai always had trouble making ends meet, but suddenly, it found itself in dire circumstances with bills piled high, financial obligations that would not go away, and more members dropping out than joining.

In 1931, one outstanding obligation was to the architect of 4th and New Hampshire, Samuel Tilden Norton. Norton and his partner, Frederick Wallis, had advanced $3,000 of their own money toward the construction of the temple, for which the board signed a note. The temple was constructed in 1925, consecrated in 1926, and had been in active use for several years already, so it was not unreasonable for Norton and Wallis to press for payment. No doubt the economic depression had affected them as it had other professionals.

But the temple could not honor its commitment and when Norton took it upon himself to approach the board to rectify the problem, he did not receive a satisfactory response. After his repeated attempts over several years to resolve the matter, and after much stalling on the part of the temple—including several personal appeals to him by board members asking him to wait just a little longer—Norton filed a lawsuit.

Norton did not belong to the temple: he was Orthodox, and the son of a very prominent member of the Los Angeles Jewish community. For one Jew to sue another in public court was not only newsworthy, it was a *shande*, a scandal or a shame. To sue a leading Jewish congregation was unprecedented.

It was no less audacious for the synagogue's directors to assume they could get away without fully paying, or in this case, repaying the architect who built their synagogue. Norton eventually won a civil judgment against the temple for the entire sum, plus attorney fees and interest. The total amounted to almost $4,000. When confronted with the verdict, Sinai attempted, even then, to persuade Norton to settle the matter for only half of what his judgment awarded. Not surprisingly, Norton rejected the offer. Eventually he received full repayment, many years after the project's completion.

At the same time as Norton was suing the temple, Rabbi Winkler also filed suit against it for nonpayment of his fees. Once again, Sinai procrastinated and then repeatedly offered to settle the rabbi's note for far less than face value. Unlike Norton, Rabbi Winkler decided to take what he could and be done with it.

He went on to create the People's Free Community Temple in Los Angeles, a house of worship that charged a $6 annual membership fee (and then only if congregants could afford it), and operated on a pay-as-you-go basis. Worship services were held in various halls for some time—one location was the Wilshire Ebell Theatre.

The rabbi earned his living performing life cycle events for which his congregants paid what they could. Significantly, Rabbi Winkler passionately believed that all Jewish children were entitled to a proper Jewish education, regardless of whether or not their families could afford it. At his new temple, he put this belief into action.

Despite the fact that Rabbi Winkler parted ways with Sinai rather acrimoniously, there were many congregants who publicly and proudly maintained their friendship with the Winklers, giving moral—if not financial—support to the rabbi's vision and his methods. One of those congregants was Dr. L. G. Reynolds, by then Sinai's honorary Life President, who wrote a tremendously moving and heartfelt article praising Rabbi Winkler after the rabbi's sudden death from a heart attack (he also had severe asthma) at the age of 62 in 1944.

In this memorial tribute, Dr. Reynolds said, "[Rabbi Winkler] gave ample evidence of his strength of character, his enormous inexhaustible energy, his effective organizing ability and, above all, his stubborn reluctance to accept unwarranted dictation from lay leaders, who felt that their monetary contributions entitled

Dr. L. G. Reynolds. President 1919–1929

them to control both the spiritual and financial policies of the Congregation."

It is clear from Dr. Reynolds' words that even with the passage of time, he did not agree with the actions of Congregation Sinai's board of directors in dismissing Rabbi Winkler. More remarkable is that he would publicly chastise his own Sinai "family" while still continuing to support it and help it grow. This quality of outspoken independence tempered with great love and indulgence is but one measure of Dr. Reynolds' stature and exemplifies why he was considered one of Sinai Temple's greatest leaders.

Survival of the Fittest

As it was for the entire country in the 1930s, money was the overriding and defining issue for the synagogue. Salaries and bank notes were deferred or unpaid. Congregation Sinai had many unsung heroes—employees, teachers, clergy—who went without for themselves and their own families so that worship wasn't suspended and students could continue their education. Monthly invoices for water, gas, and urgent repair work were paid, but anything else that could be postponed, was. All long-term financial agreements were renegotiated for *even further* extended repayment.

One might be tempted, in hindsight, to cast judgment on the people who ran the synagogue during those years. One might conclude they didn't always act responsibly in terms of honoring debt and maintaining a stellar reputation. Certainly, how one conducts business is of paramount importance in Judaism, and while no excuse should be made for how the temple treated Mr. Norton and Rabbi Winkler, it is worthwhile to note the context, that is, the Depression years.

The times were tough; they were extraordinary. Bank accounts evaporated. Basic food cost more than many people could afford. Homes were repossessed.

People did what they had to do to stay alive. Many of today's congregants at Sinai understand, firsthand, the flexibility and creativity required to endure traumatic events beyond one's control. With that in mind, and viewing history through a more charitable looking glass, it is truly amazing that Congregation Sinai actually managed, albeit barely, to remain solvent during one of the most economically trying times in U.S. history. The leadership that accomplished this great effort deserves credit.

Wanted: One Rabbi, Willing to Stay

During this time, Rabbi Max H. Kert stepped in as the congregation's next spiritual leader. From all indications, he did a terrific job. It was clear to him and all concerned that his was an interim appointment—he was there to conduct and perform services until the temple selected and hired a permanent rabbi.

The search led to an outstanding young rabbi from Dallas, whom the board greatly admired and seriously considered hiring. The only problem, which he exacerbated by writing a letter to emphasize his viewpoint, was that he didn't approve of the organ (the brand-new organ installed only four years earlier! ... the one that was bigger and better than the one at 12th and Valencia, ... and the same one that would eventually be moved to Wilshire and Beverly Glen), and he felt it should not be used. Based upon that letter alone, the board immediately dropped his candidacy. Sinai was, and to this day remains, synonymous with organ music.

As they looked for a new rabbi, the congregation's financial woes mounted. The board faced a classic dilemma: they needed to raise money (possibly through increased membership and dues), but couldn't ask congregants to pay more if there was nothing to show for it. Wisely, several board members pointed out that hiring a new and permanent rabbi would be the best "asset" to stimulate growth and justify an increase in dues.

Accordingly, the search committee refocused its attention on another candidate, a respected rabbi from New York: Dr. Jacob Kohn. He had no problem with the organ, but there was one concern: Dr. Kohn, whom they all endorsed, would be leaving a congregation in New York City that also was in dire circumstances. (Archival documents do not identify their nature, but nowhere were any aspersions cast upon the rabbi.)

The board spent time considering why Dr. Kohn would choose not to fix his own temple's problems, but would rather tackle Sinai's instead. Dr. Kohn explained, and the board accepted the explanation, that given the choice of repairing one of two "broken" congregations, he would rather put his energies into something new and personally challenging. For him, this meant coming to California.

Board president Ben Platt told the board the terms for hiring Rabbi Kohn: a $10,000 annual guarantee. Not surprisingly, when the board finally voted on the future rabbi's salary, that figure was reduced to between $6,000 and $7,000 after countless hours of discussion. Patiently, but firmly, Mr. Platt reminded them that he had guaranteed $10,000.

"Guaranteed" income was a new concept for the board, which is why the members struggled at first to understand it. Eventually, they settled upon offering the rabbi $8,000, and agreed to let him charge separately for performing bar mitzvot, weddings, funerals, and such. If those additional fees did not bring his salary up to $10,000, then Sinai would pay the difference; and, if his salary ultimately exceeded $10,000, he would not have to reimburse the temple.

With the terms of the guarantee in place, the board quickly made a formal offer to Rabbi Jacob Kohn. Rabbi Kohn was installed in the fall of 1931—not a moment too soon. Like almost every other religious institution and business at the time, the temple was on the verge of financial collapse.

Greater Than the Sum of Its Parts

In an effort to find a solution, the board examined many options. One unusual suggestion was to join forces with another congregation that also needed financial fortification. But Congregation Sinai was the only Conservative congregation in town, so joining up with another house of worship was not really an option unless they could find one willing to become either more or less religious.

It just so happened that Congregation Emmanu-El, a Reform congregation, also found itself in financial trouble as a result of the Depression. Furthermore, it had become a congregation in search of its own identity. Although it was Reform in name, the congregation actually leaned toward Conservative Judaism.

One of Sinai's former rabbis, Rabbi Liknaitz, had become a rabbi there, and it is quite possible that his influence caused a shift in the nature of their worship.

Regardless of how it happened, a few Sinai members discretely began discussions with key players at Congregation Emmanu-El about the possibility of joining forces. Why should two Jewish houses of worship fail when they could amalgamate into one stronger unit that could serve the needs of both?

This is, indeed, what happened in January of 1932. It is important to note that the minutes of the Sinai board meetings leading up to this, and all other paperwork related to this transaction, pointedly do not use the word "merger" to describe this event. In fact, all documentation strongly refutes the very notion that these two temples "merge." There are good reasons for this.

The two congregations had significant differences between them, some of which were easier to address than others. For example, Reform congregation Emmanu-El readily agreed to adopt and adhere to the doctrine and rituals of Conservative Congregation Sinai, which included ostensibly easy changes, such as wearing *kippot* and *talit*. However, the prayer books the two groups used were different; switching over, or rather, finding something that suited each temple's temperament was not so simple.

Further challenges included the fact that each of the congregations was in serious financial straits. The leaders of both temples determined that Congregation Sinai would acquire the assets of Congregation Emmanu-El. Through its amalgamation, Emmanu-El would no longer exist, which would likely cause some of its debt to be canceled. To cover the rest, Sinai could sell off Emmanu-El's remaining hard assets, such as silverware, dishes, desks, chairs, and such. But in joining forces with Sinai, the lay leadership of Emmanu-El required assurance that they would not, in any way, be trading off their own debt to somehow assume Sinai's, which was even greater.

Benjamin Platt to the Rescue

The amalgamation was accomplished in a straightforward fashion, and the new board organized easily due to the clear thinking of President Platt. Everyone on the existing board of Congregation Sinai tendered his resignation, and that board was formally dissolved. As a group of unaffiliated people, they selected Benjamin Platt as the new president of the new and larger Congregation Sinai. Its board would remain the same size as before, but would consist of an equal number of members from the "old" Congregation Sinai and from the former Congregation Emmanu-El.

Presidents Benjamin Platt, 1930–1951 (left) and Herman Platt, 1962–1964

Mr. Platt then asked these Sinai men to select three men from among themselves to help him pick a new board of half as many people as before. With half the old Sinai board about to be displaced, Mr. Platt feared that some former "big shots" might become disgruntled, having lost their power within the temple, so he wisely asked all of them to swear an oath of loyalty and support for the new endeavor. Without everyone's support, the temple would founder.

He also asked two men from the former Emmanu-El board to help select potential board members from that congregation. There was much ado about assuring the new board members from Emmanu-El that they would not become *personally* liable for existing Sinai debt. This was important because Sinai was a corporation and corporate officers typically do pledge some measure of financial responsibility for an organization on whose board they serve. Ultimately, it was decided that as new and full-fledged members of the amalgamated temple, they potentially would be liable only for future debt incurred.

Without too much trauma, Mr. Platt assembled a brand-new, blended board that everyone hoped would lead Congregation Sinai out of the wilderness of debt and depression into what they prayed would be a bright and prosperous future.

The first joint Shabbat service was held on Friday night, January 29, 1932, and a formal announcement was made the same day in the *Los Angeles Times* that Congregation Sinai and Congregation

Emmanu-El had amalgamated to form one new and more dynamic congregation, to be called—naturally—Congregation Sinai.

The banks did eventually call in their notes—which by then were long overdue—and Ben Platt appealed to them for leniency on behalf of Sinai. Adamant for repayment—even partial repayment at reduced interest rates—the banks finally refused to extend any more credit. Mr. Platt carefully considered his options as president of the congregation. He loved Congregation Sinai more than almost anything else in the world. It was an unimaginable situation, almost without remedy.

People still remember that when Mr. Platt met with the creditors, he calmly called their bluff. He handed them the deed and keys to the temple, and simply said with a big smile, "Congratulations, gentlemen, you just bought yourselves a big *shul*!" Needless to say, that is not what the bankers wanted to hear, let alone to own, and so once again they managed to work out a mutually agreeable repayment plan.

All of this took place within the first six months of Rabbi Kohn's arrival. The big-name rabbi had nearly been eclipsed by the big news happening all around him. He had been advised of the precarious nature of the temple prior to joining it, but he had not anticipated such a wild and intense transition. Letters that he wrote to family, friends, and colleagues all begged their indulgence, so thoroughly distracted and busy was he by the upheaval that coincided with his arrival.

In early 1932, 26 years after its inception, Congregation Sinai experienced a rebirth, and once again began to grow.

Dr. Jacob Kohn

Chapter Five

Survival Through the Depression

Rabbi Kohn's presence at Congregation Sinai seemed to effect remarkable change. While he was slight of stature and modest, his extraordinary charisma, undeniable strength of character, and energy galvanized people. He reinvigorated hope for the future and faith in the Almighty at a time when every visible means of proof indicated otherwise.

Los Angeles's economy was in a shambles during the Depression. Not only did the City of Angels need to keep afloat in the face of severe shortages and extreme deprivation, but its elected officials also had to adjust for, and assimilate, the hordes of people who kept moving west expecting to find work, which consistently failed to materialize.

Barely Holding On

Members of the congregation endured financial hardship and emotional distress like everyone everywhere, but the vibrant and optimistic Rabbi Kohn helped keep spirits high by focusing on the future. In his oft reprinted treatise called "The Synagogue As A Factor in Social Living," Dr. Kohn posited,

> *In this age of social disintegration through which we are passing, men are asking seriously, "Whence shall come my help?" They will not seek the answer in religion or in the social forces organized under its aegis, unless it becomes clear that the subject matter with which religion deals is the "stuff" as that in which life today finds itself so woefully entangled.*

Dr. Kohn recognized that the synagogue needed relevance in the lives of its congregants. Real issues had to be addressed seriously in order to earn and maintain credibility in the eyes of temple members.

In the 1930s, the most vexing issue for the country was, obviously, money. The synagogue, too, needed a great deal to remain solvent and functioning, and yet most of its congregants had little, if any, to give. People created their own financial priorities, and with the tightening of belts came the elimination of everything but life's necessities. While a compelling argument could be made that a relationship with God was, is, and always will be essential, it was a tough sell when there was no milk for babies, no electricity, no heat. Many, many families dropped their Sinai membership.

Many others tried their hardest to hold on. Members frequently asked the board to reduce annual dues. Among themselves, the board acknowledged that some members were taking advantage of "the times," but they knew most were not. Sporadically, the board was asked to reduce annual dues well below the minimum because of extreme financial hardship.

Allowing someone to maintain his or her dignity, the board would, occasionally, reject the appeal for dues reduction and simply waive them "until such time as the congregant could resume full payment"—knowing full well it might never happen for some. And at the same time as it showed compassion to desperate members, the temple took out yet more loans to survive and pay for its expensive new building.

To help offset the loss of income from depleted membership, Rabbi Kohn did his part to recruit new members. He set a public goal of achieving total membership of 500 by Passover. While ultimately this didn't happen, the rabbi charged all current members with bringing at least one new individual or family to the Sinai family before the spring. Furthermore, he often made personal calls and paid visits to congregants who had decided to leave the temple, asking them to reconsider. Thanks to his personal intervention, some came back.

Words of Wisdom at Sinai

For those who were able to remain at Sinai, the early 1930s brought many distinguished guest speakers. In 1932 alone—the year the Olympics came to Los Angeles and Wilshire Boulevard was paved west beyond Fairfax Avenue—Congregation Sinai engaged, among others, two prominent people to speak about the importance of Zionism.

One was a young Nobel Prize winner who would later be offered the first presidency of Israel: Albert Einstein. The other, a very passionate Golda Myerson, would many years hence change her name to Golda Meir and become one of Israel's outspoken prime ministers.

Rabbi Kohn, facilitating these lectures, easily wove his way into the heart of the entire community and soon, in his own right, became a highly sought-after orator at Jewish and secular events locally.

Sinai Schools and Mr. A. M. Tonnis

Despite the luster that such speakers brought to Sinai, the temple struggled to stay afloat. Teachers still bore the brunt of Sinai's financial woes, perhaps because as a group they comprised—and still do—the largest proportion of the payroll. They weren't paid all they were owed or according to any fixed schedule, but A. M. Tonnis (who continued to lead the educational program at Sinai) made sure everyone was paid something.

Each year, to his lasting credit, Mr. Tonnis submitted to the board a detailed, written report on the state of the schools. These are some of the best and only sources of authoritative information that chart the development of the schools during Sinai's early years.

Men's Club (Brotherhood) and Sisterhood

Records indicate that Sinai only had the vestiges of a Men's Club, or Brotherhood, by the time Rabbi Kohn arrived. Board minutes mention it briefly in 1931, when it was called Brotherhood and Mr. S. A. Miller was its president. For a short while, there was even a Young Men's

Brotherhood with an age limit of 25, later raised to 28.

Rabbi Kohn was always concerned about the morale of the congregation and firmly believed a strong Brotherhood would help assure the temple's welfare. He encouraged the men to reorganize this group that had floundered for several years.

He also gave genuine support to the Sisterhood in all of its endeavors. The Sisterhood truly deserves credit for its tangible role in the temple's sustenance throughout the Depression and its economic recovery afterwards. For over 100 years (Mrs. Emil Kornfeld is listed as its first president in 1905), it has consistently, generously, and cheerfully donated significant amounts of money toward Sinai's operating costs and programming through luncheons, theatre parties, and numerous other fundraising initiatives that continue today.

Around the World

By early 1933, domestically and around the world, much happened. The planet Pluto was discovered; "The Star-Spangled Banner" became our national anthem; and, in his landmark 1933 inaugural address, President Franklin Delano Roosevelt reminded us, "We have nothing to fear but fear itself."

As the year ended and the economic crisis continued, the majority of social services provided by the city of Los Angeles faltered. Not surprisingly, Jews were blamed, and anti-Semitism, already well-established, began to increase. The Jewish community rallied and increased its donations to organizations that employed Jews and/or provided lifeline services to them.

One such place was Cedars of Lebanon Hospital. Local anti-Semitism caused many physicians not based at the hospital to lose their practices. Still wanting (and needing) to work, they naturally turned to one of the only places that would hire Jewish doctors. In addition, the hospital patient load had increased because many Jews who could no longer afford regular health care still wanted to be treated by a Jewish doctor when they fell ill. Clearly, it benefited the greater Jewish community for this hospital to remain open and accommodate the new doctors and their patients.

By 1934, board minutes indicate that temple directors demonstrated an earnest attempt to make good on Sinai's arrears. Rabbi Kohn played an important role in this turnaround: his enthusiasm for his work and the opportunities for the advancement of Conservative Judaism motivated the board to perform at its highest level.

FDR's assessment about fear and the economy seemed insightful, at least domestically, but the unstable economies of Europe and Asia offered much to fear in terms of resultant political upheaval.

When Adolf Hitler took the title "Fuehrer" (leader) in 1934, Jews and their businesses had already suffered a major boycott in Germany, and the Nazi regime started to enforce book burnings. Many internationally renowned artists and scientists had to secret their work, and themselves, out of the country. The mass exodus of brainpower—much of it Jewish—made its way to America, and these refugees' warnings first alerted the U.S. Jewish community to the real threat facing their European kin.

In spite of firsthand reports, most Americans paid scant attention initially to the darkening news from overseas, too preoccupied with the Depression at home and what was happening in their own back yard.

Sinai stopped selling seats for the High Holidays and implemented a new membership structure referred to as "One member, one seat." (Families still had to purchase seats for their children.) This time period also marked the beginning of a long running debate over the practice of "*schnoddering*"—directly soliciting contributions in the sanctuary from those men given *aliyahs* and then announcing the amount from the pulpit. The board decided to terminate it, but, in truth, *schnoddering* continued for a few more years.

The "Small *Shul*"

The board minutes of 1934 refer to a "Small *Shul*." Never mentioned anywhere else or clearly explained, it seems, from context, that a small splinter group of Sinai congregants regularly prayed together at 4th and New Hampshire ... *and their service was Orthodox!* They paid lower dues than the rest of the congregation, and the board happily accommodated these worshippers since they contributed to the temple's bottom line.

Technically, the Small *Shul* answered to the board, and one dedicated board member, David Cohn, oversaw its activity for years. It is unclear from the minutes exactly what he did, but he regularly received great praise in board meetings, and when he died suddenly after a brief illness in 1934, everyone was heartbroken.

Occasionally, the board tried to impose various rules and regulations upon these *daveners*. However, in 1934, in a blatant attempt to entice them to pray in the main sanctuary on Shabbat mornings—giving that service the appearance of

greater popularity—the board voted to eliminate using the organ during that service out of deference to their Orthodoxy!

This appears to be the *only* time the temple made *any* concession to *anyone* regarding the organ. Unfortunately, the gambit failed, and again, for reasons unclear, the board subsequently decided to discontinue Sinai membership through the Small *Shul*. While it terminated Shabbat Orthodox services, Sinai still continued to offer Orthodox High Holiday services for its former Small *Shul* members.

Another milestone event, which occurred in 1935, was that KMTR Radio asked Rabbi Kohn to broadcast a portion of his weekly Shabbat service on one of their community religious programs. The rabbi happily agreed. One can only wonder if this caused any friction or merely piqued the competitive spirit with his rabbinic colleague and friend, Rabbi Isidore Myers, who was the first rabbi in town to broadcast on radio and who still had his own program.

The economy began to pick up slightly in 1936 and a renewed sense of generosity blossomed among its inhabitants. Ever ready to work on behalf of the temple, Sisterhood proposed and orchestrated the first annual dinner-dance that year. It took place in the Cocoanut Grove Ballroom at the Ambassador Hotel, with an ad journal to commemorate the celebration and raise money. Sinai continues to hold these annual membership-wide galas, raising money to supplement vital programs and activities for which Sinai is known. On alternating years, the dinner honors the outgoing board president or outstanding congregants.

Several different philanthropic organizations were founded in 1936, many of which still exist today. Significantly, and with the support of the entire community, the Bureau of Jewish Education was established to coordinate and oversee Jewish education by establishing standards and goals for juveniles and adults.

One thing people at Sinai didn't support was the ongoing and controversial tradition of *schnoddering*. Supposedly discontinued in 1934, the practice never abated. The board finally and officially moved to abolish it forever. Once they did, many members expressed concern that a vital source of income would disappear. To circumvent this, the temple gave a preprinted donation card to every man receiving an *aliyah*, trusting he would have the good sense to show his gratitude.

When it came to gratitude, no one had more than Rabbi Kohn when the Men's Club, after years of inactivity, finally reorganized. Later that year, around the High Holidays, in another effort to promote the temple's welfare and further its outreach, the synagogue offered Junior Temple memberships to singles and young married couples, hoping to bring them into the Sinai fold.

A very well-educated and well-spoken single young man named David I. Lippert joined in 1936 because he was absolutely enthralled by Dr. Kohn's scholarship and oratorical skill. Mr. Lippert paid $15 in annual dues, and for Sinai's "investment" in this promising new member, he eventually became one of its most generous and influential members, and also, because of his virtue, one of its most beloved.

In 1937, with so many serious matters still at hand, the temple made a great to-do over *kippot*. The board decided men should no longer wear street hats in the sanctuary, but instead, a uniform, dark skullcap. Such a radical change necessitated many meetings about where men's hats would be stored, how many different sizes of *kippot* should be ordered, where they should be placed, and how they would be kept clean (hair tonics and oils were popular back then).

Grave Matters

For a while, men's fashion seemed a life-or-death issue. But the temple's financial health, as always, brought everyone back to reality. For nearly three years, several gentlemen on the board had tried to negotiate for Congregation Sinai to own a cemetery.

In April, they finally struck a mutually satisfactory arrangement with the Home of Peace Cemetery, only to have it fall through soon thereafter, for reasons not explained in the minutes. Leaders turned to B'nai B'rith Temple to try to strike a similar deal. But that temple rejected the existing terms and insisted on starting all over. It was a huge disappointment to everyone involved.

Then, in August, Security-First National Bank of Los Angeles, Sinai's mortgage holder, sent a letter indicating they would foreclose on the property in November for chronic lack of payment. While greatly improved in its day-to-day fiscal operations, Sinai was still behind on mortgage and interest payments, a tab that came to an extraordinary $228,881.48!

A frantic fundraising appeal began. L. K. Shapiro, a well-known thoroughbred racehorse owner, organized (and led) a banking committee to plead for leniency from Security-First National and negotiate a settlement. It was a very difficult assignment because Sinai's bankers had finally run out of patience.

One of Sinai's options was to do nothing until the foreclosure sale in

At the December 1937 annual congregational meeting, a delightful 6-year-old boy named Lorin Maazel played violin selections for the congregants' entertainment. Today, he is the internationally renowned music director of the New York Philharmonic!

November. The temple could try to re-purchase its own building at auction, hoping to have enough money to outbid any competitors. The strategy was extremely risky and a long shot, and didn't appeal to Mr. Shapiro, a reasonable risk-taker by nature, with a fine-tuned intuition for long shots.

Sinai could not have picked a better "jockey" for this critical race. Mr. Shapiro skillfully negotiated a 10-year settlement that was slightly less favorable than Sinai had hoped for, but at a better interest rate than they had anticipated ... saving 4th and New Hampshire by a nose.

To seal the deal, the first money had to be delivered almost immediately. Even with all the money they had raised, the temple coffers still had insufficient funds. Mr. Sam Serber, a long-time member and director, wrote a check for $4,000 on the spot when he was informed of the crisis and truly saved the day. In gratitude, the synagogue made a dinner especially in his honor shortly thereafter, equally celebrating Mr. Shapiro.

"I Am My Brother's Keeper"

The next year, 1938, progressed rather uneventfully at the temple. The same could not be said elsewhere. By December, Herman A. Bachrack took a moment to "digress" at a board meeting from Sinai's business at hand to express sympathy for his co-religionists overseas. He was referring to *Kristallnacht* (Night of Broken Glass, November 9 and 10) in Germany and Austria, during which Nazis smashed all the windows of, and also looted and burned, Jewish synagogues, businesses, and homes.

Only three years before at the annual congregational meeting on December 14, 1935, Dr. Kohn seemed to have had a prescient vision of the future when he uttered these words:

> *"As we view the spread of anti-Semitism, as we witness the futility of Jewish protests throughout the world, and we realize that what our fathers said, at least for the Jews of the Diaspora, is true—'Naught is left us save this Torah alone'—there is no other strength excepting in our faith which makes it worthwhile to remain Jews. The Jew who loses that will have to fight as well as the Jew who has it."*

The board minutes from the 1938 meeting do not reflect any further discussion or recommended course of action at that time in response to *Kristallnacht*, either as a congregation or as part of the Jewish community, but Dr. Kohn's message about the perils of increasing anti-Semitism took on new significance for those paying attention.

The Decade Comes to a Close

The decade ended on a better note than it began for the premier Conservative congregation of the West Coast. In 1939, in recognition of Mr. Tonnis's excellence as an educator and as a reflection of his stature within the Jewish community, the Bureau of Jewish Education offered him a part-time position as principal of the Los Angeles Jewish Academy. By the Bureau's own definition, it had to be secondary to his responsibilities at Sinai.

Initially, this highly unusual arrangement stumped the Sinai board, whose members weren't sure if holding both jobs simultaneously created a conflict of interest. They also questioned whether their own schools would suffer for lack of his full attention. After much consideration, they gave Mr. Tonnis their blessing.

Separately, but also perplexing, in that same year, the United Synagogue Kashruth Organization asked to visit Sinai to explain their purpose and meet with members. Although the board sent them a warm letter of welcome, it is not certain if Mrs. Fradelis, Sinai's unofficial kosher caterer of longstanding, felt the same way. Furthermore, Sisterhood, which had run all Sinai kitchens since their inception, took umbrage. It considered the request an insinuation that Sisterhood didn't keep kosher to the highest standards, which it did. Most likely, the visit was an outreach mission to encourage more families to keep kosher, in and out of the home.

And just to keep things interesting, *schnoddering* was reinstated.

Looking Forward into the 1940s

The country's economy began to recover from the harrowing Depression, and so, too, did Sinai's. The board of directors started running the temple like a business, balancing its budget and spending only what it had, nothing more. The temple had installed a dynamic rabbi who brought honor to his flock, inspired everyone who met him, and who rigorously promoted Conservative Judaism and all that it stood for.

For Jews across Europe and Russia, however, life became more difficult and dangerous, but few anywhere could truly imagine what was yet to come. Only a short time would pass before the shadow of World War II took shape as a squadron of planes over Pearl Harbor. Until then, Congregation Sinai could be proud of the fact that it still stood at 4th and New Hampshire, offering spiritual sanctuary for Jews in the City of Angels.

The Burning of the Mortgage - 4th & New Hampshire
Theodore Strimling
Emil Brown
Adolf Weinberg
Ben Platt

Chapter Six

Taking Care of Business at Home

In May 1940, the directors passed a motion to send a letter from the board to the congregation alerting them to the dire need of "our people overseas," urging them to contribute money to the Jewish Welfare Fund campaign to the very limit of their financial ability.

Cantor Silverman's Swan Song

As the High Holidays approached, Sinai's on-again/off-again Small *Shul* once again offered Orthodox services, with Samuel Goldman conducting. At the same time, Cantor Silverman—who had been plagued by a variety of recurrent illnesses over the years—became very seriously ill, prompting the board to gently suggest he hire an assistant cantor for the Holidays. The board was genuinely afraid that too much singing

would damage the cantor's voice and impair a complete recovery.

On December 2, 1940, to the profound sorrow of everyone at Sinai and throughout the Jewish community, beloved Cantor Abraham Silverman succumbed. His dignified funeral took place in the synagogue, but the war precluded an official memorial until November 21, 1941—his *yahrzeit*. The Cantors' Association meeting was in town and performed an impressive musical program for that Friday night service.

As a gesture of compassion and respect for the late cantor and his widow, the board voted to pay Cantor Silverman's widow (for whom no other financial provisions had been made) a small monthly stipend for a period of one year, along with a seat in the temple for the rest of her life. They later extended the stipend in perpetuity. (It would be several more years before life insurance, pensions, and other sophisticated financial vehicles became standard for temple employees.)

Also at this time, to show respect for members of the community who had been drafted recently—and hadn't yet left—or would soon be drafted, the temple allotted twenty seats so they could pray in advance of leaving.

To replace the cantor, Sinai interviewed two people. Following an outstanding audition in the home of Ben Platt on February 19, 1941, the board offered Leib Glantz a one-year contract as cantor and musical director at a salary of $300 a month. Before joining Congregation Sinai, he had made concert tours through Mexico, Canada, England, South Africa, Russia, and Romania, and had performed services in the major synagogues in Israel (then Palestine), where he also gave numerous concerts.

Cantor Glantz immigrated to the United States in 1927. He was by then a popular recording artist, singing in both Hebrew and Yiddish on the Victor/Red Seal label, and an authority on Jewish sacred music. As he said, "My great work is to so transcribe traditional music into modern form because the new trend has to be illustrated by the music and I make old compositions new."

Considering the Future

By May 1941, Congregation Sinai returned to the idea of purchasing its own cemetery. Nothing had come of any previous attempts, and the temple wanted to try again. The board gave Vice President Theodore Strimling permission to approach the cemetery committee of Wilshire Boulevard Temple to see if he might strike a deal.

Children's assembly to mourn the passing of President Franklin Delano Roosevelt.

At the same time, Mr. Strimling and a few other forward-thinking members also resuscitated the idea of, and began aggressively lobbying for, opening a western branch of the school. Attendance in Sinai's schools had dropped off in the previous year because members who had started moving west and away from 4th and New Hampshire didn't want to drive far to take their children to school. Mr. Strimling recognized the imperative to stanch this outflow before it seriously affected the schools' and the temple's viability.

Whereas the schools' support lagged, the Sunday Morning Sinai Forum for adults drew great attendance and praise. It featured guest speakers on topics ranging from current events to politics to issues of concern to the Jewish community, and included a question-and-answer period followed by group discussion. One of the unexpected results of Forum attendance was that it inspired congregants to increase their overall reading—making them highly informed about numerous subjects, as well as fine conversationalists, too.

Just as Rabbi Winkler had been instrumental in organizing interfaith dialogue and activities throughout the city, Rabbi Kohn also adopted the role of

community builder in Los Angeles, trying to bring different peoples together to heal the world. He served as a member of the World Conference on Religion, which was comprised of a group of clergymen, scientists, and philosophers whose idealistic goal was to lay the foundation for world democracy.

However, by mid-1941, the progressively desperate situation of European Jewry became one of Rabbi Kohn's greatest concerns. Long before the issue caught fire in the minds of the mainstream Jewish community, he spoke of the need to support Jewish brethren overseas, whose plight worsened daily. Those in the United States who knew the Nazis were doing terrible things tried to prevent further harm. But with no one in real power in the United States willing to listen and seriously help (with the exception of Treasury Secretary Henry Morgenthau Jr.), they couldn't get enough done to make a real difference in time.

The War Years

On December 7, 1941, Japanese planes attacked the U.S. naval fleet stationed in Pearl Harbor, Hawaii, and the United States officially entered the Second World War. At Congregation Sinai's annual membership meeting only two days later, scant mention was made of the attack—at least in the minutes—but Rabbi Kohn did say, "There is no larger movement in the world today for world justice than the Jewish religion." In his eyes, all Jews needed to do more, and the United States, as a nation, definitely needed to do more to rescue the Jews.

Los Angeles Jews did not shirk their obligation to defend their homeland, and Sinai's members were no exception. As during World War I, almost every family had at least one immediate relative serving in the military. Records indicate that nearly 250 Sinai men and women served. First Lieutenant Charles I. Brown, Corporal Martin Frieze, Private Fred H. Marx, and Private Walter Stern were killed in action defending the freedom of their countrymen, and Sinai Temple will always be grateful to them and to their families for the sacrifice they made.

As the year concluded on a note of war and worry, Rabbi Kohn kept the congregation looking forward, with hope. He endorsed the idea of a Westside branch of the weekday school so Sinai's children would be well prepared for whatever their future might hold. It would still be more than a year before this dream began to materialize.

Sisterhood Responds

The war years engendered a bold spirit of social activism at the temple. Nowhere was this more apparent than in Sisterhood, forever the backbone of the congregation. In 1940, Sisterhood received the unmitigated support and long overdue acknowledgment it deserved when the board granted it a permanent seat on the board of directors in recognition of the group's unfailing commitment to the temple, and its consistent contributions. The board also decided that all sitting presidents of Sisterhood and the Men's Club, in perpetuity, should automatically receive full-fledged representation on the board.

Then, as now, Sisterhood regularly supported the work of the congregation by sponsoring and participating in numerous activities. Throughout the year on Shabbat, it purchased the pulpit flowers, as it still does. Sisterhood also purchased prayer books and biblical texts through the Perpetual Prayer Book Fund; today, it gives each bar and bat mitzvah a copy of the *High Holiday Prayer Book*.

The Only Mr. Sisterhood! One outstanding member of the congregation, Sam Smotrich, was so helpful to Sisterhood and so admired that they made him the first, and only, male life member! Today, his granddaughter Debbie Diamond is a member of Sisterhood, and her children—fourth-generation Sinai-ites!—attend Sinai schools.

Sisterhood was affiliated nationally with the Women's League of United Synagogue, and Sinai's women participated in such organizations as Hadassah, National Council of Jewish Women, the Women's Auxiliary of B'nai B'rith, the Community Chest and Welfare Fund, and the Conference of Jewish Organizations, to name but a few. In addition, several of its members sat on national boards of numerous Jewish organizations. This holds true for many of today's Sisterhood members, as well.

Sisterhood conducted regular fundraisers to assure the upkeep and maintenance of the school since its members believed that quality education best occurred in a well-maintained facility. Women also worked hard to make holidays and events throughout the year interesting and inspiring to the children. During Passover, they set the table and provided refreshments for the model seders. At Shavout for confirmation, they organized mothers to create decorations and host the party. On Sukkot, they helped decorate the *sukkah*, hosting the congregation and providing refreshments in it, and also made a party for the children. At Chanukah and Purim, they provided gifts at the school assemblies.

Sinai Sisterhood made contributions to the Chaplain's Service Corps and sponsored a weekly Red Cross unit meeting. They were represented on the Army and Navy Committee of the Jewish Welfare Board sponsoring USO events to warm the hearts of hardworking troops and, to keep them literally warm, the ladies knitted sweaters, scarves, gloves, and other needed items that they regularly sent overseas.

The women of Sisterhood took very seriously their responsibility for the spiritual soundness of the Jewish home as well as Congregation Sinai, every member's holy home away from home. Mrs. Charles Roth, president of Sisterhood from 1942–1946, expressed this sentiment perfectly: "... the Sisterhood aims to do for the synagogue what the thoughtful mother does for the home, that is to make it beautiful and inviting."

Making Sinai's Home Safe and Sound

Benjamin Platt had been president of Sinai since 1930, just shortly after the congregation moved to 4th and New Hampshire. He had led the temple carefully and creatively through many dark days. With the help of Emil Brown, Honorary Life Treasurer, Sinai had slowly gotten back on its feet financially. The temple showed increased responsibility for all its financial obligations by the end of the 1930s, whittling away at its considerable debt faithfully and on time.

The Unit of Red Cross Sisterhood met every Thursday to knit and make the bandages for those in need.

All the same, it bothered Mr. Platt, personally and professionally, that Sinai still owed money on its mortgage—about $50,000 in the early 1940s—because it meant the temple building really didn't belong to the members yet. To him, that just wasn't good business. Until the debt was retired, the banks could call in their loans if Sinai should find itself unable to make payments for any reason. In 1942, Platt suggested a major fundraising campaign to pay off the mortgage in two years.

He envisioned this campaign in two stages: first raising $30,000; then the balance of $20,000. Many people complained that all they ever did was write checks to Congregation Sinai. Mr. Platt certainly had the right to ask others for money because he was always first to contribute and had personally renegotiated the temple's mortgage several times in the past to keep the temple afloat.

The first target was quickly met. The second actually became easier to reach when the amount being sought shrank; miraculously, various creditors, including Union Bank and Trust Company, forgave all or part of their loans to Sinai as good-faith gestures to help pay off the mortgage.

> In the words of Mr. Eugene M. Rosen, one of Sinai's most dedicated members who served in numerous capacities on the Board over many years, the burning of Sinai's mortgage "is announcing to the world that its membership, even at a time of international crisis, has not forgotten those deeper values which govern life; it is saying quite plainly that its members recognize that the synagogue must continue to be a 'place of many mansions,' to which all can come and from which all can receive an understanding of those moral values without which a decent society cannot exist."

Emil Brown

To each time period comes a hero. Just as Ben Platt saved the day nearly 20 years earlier when the temple needed funds to complete construction at 4th and New Hampshire—which Emil Brown had vigilantly supervised, making sure plans were followed, budgets adhered to, and salaries paid—that same Mr. Brown turned out to be such a champion in the temple's quest to burn its mortgage.

No one was surprised that he contributed a generous sum of money toward the mortgage's retirement. However, the actual amount was so generous (although not specified in the minutes) that he almost single-handedly assured the temple's financial freedom. Had he not already been honored with the title "Honorary Life Treasurer," he surely would have deserved it based on this alone.

It took almost a year after the mortgage was officially redeemed for the synagogue to hold a commemorative ceremony. The directors wanted to mark the occasion with an event, or a series of events, that celebrated the accomplishment in triumph, but the war still raged, placing many Sinai sons, daughters, fathers, and husbands directly in harm's way. It didn't seem fitting to rejoice yet.

In fact, many secular practices that had become routine at Sinai prior to the outbreak of war no longer seemed appropriate. For example, for nearly a decade, the temple held an annual fundraising dinner-dance for its members. In wartime 1943, Mr. Platt suggested an evening of opera instead. While still entertaining, music alone seemed less festive than dancing. The temple bought out a performance of the visiting San Carlos Opera Company for $2,500. The evening was a success, and the temple repeated the formula for the remaining war years.

Finally, on May 30, 1945—with the war in Europe won, but the war in Japan not done—Congregation Sinai held a formal mortgage-burning ceremony and gala. Over 300 people watched as Ben Platt held the mortgage deed aloft and Emil Brown torched it. Rabbi Kohn chanted the *Shehecheyonu* just as the flames took hold and Cantor Glantz led the choir in a musical program.

The temple commissioned a beautiful book called *Sinai,* written by member Charles Jacobson, to commemorate the event and relate the synagogue's history from 1909–1945. (That book proved invaluable in the research for, and creation of, this book.) At last, the focus of the temple could move from mere survival to true growth, and programs and projects long delayed could begin to be implemented.

Shortly after the burning of the mortgage, the war in Japan ended. Rabbi Kohn anticipated the trauma experienced by the returning soldiers, and he frequently spoke to the congregants of the need to help veterans, especially the younger ones, readjust to "normal" life and overcome the war horrors they had witnessed. But "normal" would never again be the same for anyone after Auschwitz, Dachau, Hiroshima, and Nagasaki.

Los Angeles gratefully welcomed home its sons and daughters, and the temple mourned with those families who lost loved ones. While Sinai's membership had grown steadily through the war years, the directors always, and wisely, had reserved space for returning veterans so they could immediately resume worship in their regular seats. In short order, they did, and soon the sanctuary brimmed with joy and life once again.

Mortgage burning at Park Manor Caterers

Eva and John Ziegler

Chapter Seven

Regrouping After the War

A spirit of renewal came over the country as it recovered from the war. Los Angeles became a destination of choice for thousands of returning soldiers who had first experienced the city's balmy winters or temperate summers en route to the Pacific war theatre. Many brought their brides; others, the families who had waited for them. In addition, the city attracted a large number of Jewish refugees. Together, the newcomers contributed to the most serious housing problem anywhere in the nation.

Sinai's First Assistant Rabbi: Jacob Pressman

By October of 1946, Sinai's membership stood at over 600 families. The growth of the temple and increasing workload prompted Rabbi Kohn to ask

From left to right: Theodore Strimling, Margie Pressman, Ben Platt, Rabbi and Mrs. Jacob Kohn, Rabbi Jacob Pressman, and Dr. Louis Finkelstein, President of the Seminary

Keeping Kosher

It is interesting to note that *kashruth* was not strictly observed outside the synagogue or members' homes at that time. Rabbi Pressman recalls that he, Rabbi Kohn, and Rabbi Solomon Goldman of Chicago, the gala celebration's guest speaker, were the only people in attendance who made advance requests for special kosher meals, which were served on airline-style wrapped trays. It would still be some time before the major hotels offered fresh kosher food as standard fare.

for an assistant rabbi. Benjamin Platt went to the Seminary in search of someone special, and Dr. Louis Finkelstein, the head of the seminary, recommended Rabbi Jacob Pressman, a talented young man then ministering to the prestigious Forest Hills Jewish Center in Forest Hills, New York.

Jacob Pressman was born at home in Philadelphia, Pennsylvania, on October 26, 1919. His parents came to the United States from Russia. His father was a traveling salesman; his mother, a homemaker. Jacob graduated from the University of Pennsylvania in 1940, Phi Beta Kappa, with honors in English literature. He became a rabbi in 1945, graduating from JTS with a prize in public speaking and the degree Master of Hebrew Letters (later, Doctor of Hebrew Letters, Honorary Doctor of Divinity, and Doctor of Humane Letters). Rabbi Jack, as he is affectionately known, speaks and reads English, Hebrew, Yiddish, French, German, and Spanish.

Rabbi Finkelstein encouraged this bright and popular young man to move to Los Angeles, predicting that the future of Conservative Judaism would rest on three world pillars: New York, Los Angeles, and Palestine. Taking these words to heart, Rabbi Pressman and his young wife, Marjorie (Margie), rushed out to Los Angeles in time for a gala celebration at the Ambassador Hotel marking Rabbi Kohn's 60th birthday.

The severe housing shortage that plagued the city seriously affected the Pressmans. For months, they bounced from one short-term rental room to another, sometimes depending on the kindness of congregants for shelter. It was frustrating and exhausting, but they were good sports. Finally, when Mrs. Pressman became pregnant with their first child, the board acknowledged that temporary quarters would no longer suffice, and the temple luckily found and bought a house for them on Oakwood Street.

Six months after the temple engaged Rabbi Pressman, Cantor Glantz resigned. Board minutes suggest that he could not convince the board to pay the salary he felt he deserved. More than that, though, it seems the cantor and the board just didn't see eye to eye on his role.

Without doubt, Sinai recognized Cantor Glantz as an excellent *Hazzan*. Cantor Glantz, however, was an internationally recognized recording artist who wanted to modernize classical Jewish liturgical music. He regularly asked the board for additional money to cover the cost of music transcription, and the board simply didn't see the need. The temple merely wanted someone knowledgeable in Jewish music and who could sing with a beautiful voice and the proper spirit. *Dayenu*.

In retrospect, Leib Glantz may have been the first "superstar" cantor of Sinai, but Sinai wasn't attuned to his vision ... or, in this case, his ear. According to Aryell Cohen, current choir director and organist at Sinai for 30 years, Cantor Glantz's original music "was and remains very avant garde sounding, and was not appreciated at the time. Of his music that is in print, some cantors and other Jewish singers will perform one of his compositions in concert, but the music is not used in synagogue worship."

While the congregation and cantor didn't mesh well, the new assistant rabbi seemed to everyone a perfect choice. He and Rabbi Kohn got along famously, falling into a kind of father–son dynamic ... and much to Rabbi Kohn's delight, he found in Rabbi Pressman a willing conversationalist during Shabbat services. They sat on the *bimah* and avidly discussed that week's Torah portion. Rabbi Kohn often surprised his young protégé with esoteric commentary and information he gleaned from unusual resources during his own study. In short time, some members—including the very proper Mr. John Ziegler, who always dressed for *shul* in a frock coat or a morning coat, striped trousers, and a high hat—complained about their private banter, so the two men had to be separated!

In addition to his pronounced taste in clothing, Mr. Ziegler had very strong political views and loathed Presidents Roosevelt and Truman. Every week during the prayer for our nation, he stood up and walked out of the sanctuary to make a clear statement of protest against our country's leaders. Every week, the rabbis waited for it.

Mr. Ziegler took great interest in the temple, and all his children eventually followed suit to some degree. His son Allen, and Allen's wife, Ruth, became two of Sinai's greatest benefactors ever.

A Post-War Welcome

After the war, Sinai opened its doors to survivors and refugees from Europe who wanted to join. Some came with little more than the clothes on their backs. The temple did everything it could to accommodate these special members and help integrate them with dignity into a new life.

Sinai Temple respects and honors holocaust survivors every day, but especially so on *Yom HaShoah*, Holocaust Remembrance Day. Holocaust-related events held at Sinai Temple are usually emotionally charged, in part because Sinai is blessed to count among its members many men and women who survived or escaped Hitler's very real nightmare.

Sinai Temple's Yom Kippur *yizkor* service includes a martyrology, which pays special tribute to all martyrs in Jewish history. During this service, many people weep, remembering grandparents, parents, children, or even ancient heroes whose innocence, or whose acts of goodness, modesty, or bravery live on in the hearts of those who cherish their memory. One year during an exceptionally moving Yom Kippur martyrology, the congregation listened, silently transfixed, to an hour of prerecorded audio during which survivors narrated their raw and amazing stories.

Sinai Young Fellowship

Typically, after wars come weddings. People married at a much younger age in the 1940s than they do today, and newlyweds in their 20s didn't mingle with "oldsters" in their 40s! Sinai found itself in need of programming for young couples, and the Sinai Young Fellowship, organized in 1947, became the place for "young marrieds" to meet and create a sense of community.

About 20 couples started the group, and others joined along the way. They met about once a month, and their activities included picnics and potluck suppers. One year at Purim, they got permission to shoot a16mm movie in front of the Christian Science Church on 8th Street; unfortunately, the film has disappeared. Rabbi Pressman encouraged eligible members to participate, including Selma and Sydney Daye, Vi and Bill Friedland, Hilda and Karl Silvers, and Ruth and Dr. David Fiske. Many have become temple and community leaders.

Extending the Friday Night Services

One of Conservative Judaism's contributions to religious expression was the introduction of a formal, extended Friday night Shabbat service. The origins of this tradition can be traced back to World War I when, as Dr. Kohn reminded his congregants, "... economic conditions make it next to impossible for many to attend Sabbath morning services." He added, "Most Conservative synagogues, including our own, have developed Friday evening devotions which begin at 8 o'clock. Even the transportation difficulties brought on by the (current) war have not interrupted these regular Sabbath devotions ... ."

Sinai members loved gathering for Friday night services to put the week behind them, forget their cares, and welcome Shabbat together. Large attendance became a deeply embedded tradition for the next 40 years, far surpassing Shabbat morning attendance.

The extended Friday night service allowed time for the rabbis to deliver a sermon of significant length and serious topic. Rabbis Kohn and Pressman alternated speaking on Friday nights, but only Rabbi Kohn orated on Shabbat morning. Typically, Rabbi Kohn's sermons con-

Augusta Kohn

cerned *divrei Torah*—their content was not sociopolitical in nature. He was a staunch proponent of the Conservative movement, still in its infancy, and often, he would focus on the innovation and beauty of Conservative Judaism—partly to reinforce it, partly to praise and validate Congregation Sinai for being in the forefront of the movement.

These sermons with their florid language, intellectual themes, and abstract concepts mesmerized the congregation, though even the smartest people often couldn't understand what Dr. Kohn meant. Once, after the erudite Rabbi Emeritus Dr. Kohn spoke, Dr. Edward Kamenir asked his successor, Rabbi Israel Chodos, to explain a particular point his elder raised in the sermon. Rabbi Chodos reportedly replied, "I would if I could fully grasp it, but it sure sounded good, didn't it?!" Even though he communicated above their heads, Sinai members loved having Jacob Kohn preach to them each week if only because he was legendary among West Coast clergy—the "best" rabbi, as if there could be such a distinction—and they loved being able to claim him as "theirs."

A Man Like No Other ... Like Everybody

For all of his scholarship and wisdom, Rabbi Kohn's personal life was, in many ways, unremarkable. As one would hope, he adored his wife and loved his children, and he had typically complex relationships with his friends and siblings. Found in the archives, personal correspondence to his children, brothers, and business associates reveals a kind man with a good sense of humor, occasionally frustrated by a lack of time resulting from increasing professional responsibilities. These letters also shed light on the rabbi's sensibility and compassion for his congregants' dilemmas about *halacha* and its interpretation in a modern world.

The Rebbitzen: Augusta Hirsch Kohn

One very special person merits mention and praise for helping Rabbi Kohn in everything he did: his wife, Augusta Hirsch Kohn. Rabbi Kohn referred to her as his "Great Lady," and said that she was too modest to seek praise and too humble to need it. Everyone genuinely loved her. Many people went to the *rebbitzen* for advice and inspiration, turning the Kohn home into a popular place for get-togethers followed by tea and cookies.

A full-time mother to three sons and a daughter, Augusta "Gus" Kohn had an impact on a far wider circle than her immediate family. She became a role model and surrogate mother to Margie Pressman as she began her own journey as a wife, mother, and *rebbitzen*. Her vital contributions to Sinai and the Los Angeles Jewish community, as well as the international Jewish community, advanced the cause of Conservative Judaism and women's role in it.

She served as president of the Conference of Jewish Women's Organizations in Los Angeles; she worked with Mrs. Solomon Schechter to organize the Sisterhoods of the Conservative Movement (which today has over 613 affiliates in the United States and Canada); and, with Henrietta Szold, she served as a member of the planning committee that founded Hadassah.

According to Selma Carow, a three-time president of Sinai's Sisterhood, "She brought added meaning and a better understanding of Jewish values to the women of our community." People who still remember this *ayshes chayel* (woman of valor) always do so with a smile on their faces and a warm and loving anecdote. Through a lifetime of *tzedakah* and *tikkun olam*, Augusta Kohn earned a lasting name for herself.

He also had a few innocent "secrets." One was that he rarely knew the bar mitzvah boys' names. Their teachers and the cantor supervised most of their preparation, and Dr. Kohn actually spent little time with each youngster. On Shabbat when he addressed the bar mitzvah on the *bimah*, he would usually greet him as "My boy," "Young man," or "My son" because it saved them both from embarrassment! Another little known "secret" was that every afternoon at four o'clock when Hebrew school started, he would slip out of the office and go home to walk his dog, thereby getting some fresh air and some time for himself.

"Rabbi Jack" Becomes a Westside Presence

Warm, gregarious, with a big smile and real *joie de vivre*, Rabbi Jack Pressman gathered admirers everywhere he went. Congregation Sinai, especially his young contemporaries and the school children, responded enthusiastically to the new assistant rabbi. Ever energetic and helpful, Rabbi Pressman also offered his expertise to many nascent temples and organizations, helping them grow. He was director of West Coast USY for quite some time, and he played a significant part in the development of Valley Jewish Community Temple and Center, which later became congregation Adat Ari El. Rabbi Kohn had no problem with Rabbi Pressman's considerable outreach activities—even leading services at other congregations—as long as they didn't interfere with his primary obligation to Sinai's schools and his regular pastoral work.

Rabbi Pressman worked closely and well with A. M. Tonnis to make the schools the very best they could be. He agreed with Theodore Strimling's earlier assessment that Sinai needed a school presence on the Westside and, with Rabbi Kohn's and Mr. Tonnis's knowledge, he began looking for undeveloped land or an existing property that could suit the school's needs. The Brentwood Academy property on eight acres at Sunset and Barrington was available, but Ben Platt pronounced the $250,000 price too high. Next, he found another available spot near Sinai's current location for $180,000. If Sinai were to acquire that, it would no doubt take a while to purchase.

At the same time, without temple leadership's knowledge, an enterprising and dedicated teacher named Miriam Freibrun began holding private classes on the porch of her Westwood home for some Sinai children. Rabbi Pressman quietly helped by overseeing her curriculum. Word spread, classes grew, and temple management learned of (and later endorsed) her subterfuge because it gave the synagogue the Westside toehold it needed for the next two years. Sinai Temple had "officially" opened a Westside school on Robertson Boulevard in Beverly Hills concurrently, but records indicate it sputtered open and closed a few times due to the fluctuating finances of the temple.

The University of Judaism: The Seminary's West Coast Branch

In 1947, Rabbi Kohn, Rabbi Pressman, Benjamin Platt, Theodore Strimling,

Aaron Gordon, and several other stalwarts of Sinai—with other prominent members of the Los Angeles Jewish community—began to volunteer countless hours and demonstrate immeasurable passion toward building a University of Judaism (UJ) in Los Angeles. This institution was originally envisioned as the West Coast branch of the Jewish Theological Seminary (JTS).

With his typical sense of humor, Rabbi Pressman is fond of saying the UJ started on his telephone. What he means is that Rabbi Kohn didn't have a phone in his office: when he joined the temple in 1931, few people had phones, the temple's rarely rang, and those people who needed to speak with Dr. Kohn usually came to see him at his office.

As the years went by and phones became thoroughly integrated into daily life, the rabbi felt no need to adapt. When someone phoned for him, his secretary would announce the caller and the reason, and Dr. Kohn would leave his office and walk over to her desk to take the call. When Rabbi Pressman arrived, he campaigned hard for his own office *with a phone*. Fortunately, he prevailed, soon using that phone to plead the cause of the UJ on behalf of the senior rabbi and himself.

The birth of the UJ is inextricably linked to Dr. Kohn and Congregation Sinai. Rabbi Kohn's position as head of a prominent Conservative congregation in the Western United States, as well as his leading role in the Rabbinic Assembly—plus the fact that he was a graduate of the Seminary in New York—made him a natural to spearhead such an enormous endeavor.

Furthermore, since he had an assistant he liked very much and with whom he could juggle responsibilities, he was in a position to divide his energies, if not his loyalties, between the new university and the temple. Rabbi Kohn invited several of Sinai's most dedicated members to direct their extra time and additional resources toward an important seat of higher learning to benefit all Jews and the study of Judaism.

The UJ was housed at Sinai for its first two years. It then moved to a house at 612 S. Ardmore. Many UJ classes and adult education functions were held at Sinai since its own facility was too small.

The fact that JTS sought to expand so significantly when it did affirms the growth and popularity of Conservative Judaism in the United States by the mid-1940s. The UJ's location in Los Angeles validated Dr. Finkelstein's prediction that

Los Angeles would become a pillar of Conservative Jewry. That Rabbis Kohn and Pressman could continue serving as dynamic a congregation as Sinai and simultaneously coordinate a project of this magnitude bears testimony to nothing less than a modern miracle.

Congregation Sinai had only recently cleared its mortgage and begun to operate in the black. In many ways, it took great *chutzpah* to turn around and ask members for money, yet again, and for a cause distinct from Sinai. But those asking gave even more of themselves than they requested of others. Rabbi Kohn not only founded the UJ, but also served as its first dean of graduate studies. Rabbi Pressman served as the registrar, and Ben Platt and others served on the board of governors and gave their hearts and souls to make the UJ one of the finest centers of Jewish learning and knowledge in the world.

Rabbi Pressman Leaves; Rabbi Lieber Presses On

In 1950, Rabbi Pressman received an offer to become senior rabbi of the Olympic Jewish Temple and Center, a young and growing congregation that later became Temple Beth Am. He is their rabbi emeritus today. His departure surprised and saddened the congregation, which held him in high esteem and valued his friendship. Rabbi Kohn, especially, took his decision hard because, in addition to his great personal affection for Rabbi Pressman, he had grown accustomed to having an associate. He took comfort in knowing that the two of them would still have plenty of opportunity to interact, especially through their affiliation with the UJ.

Dr. Kohn needed another assistant rabbi, so Ben Platt hired Rabbi David Lieber. Rabbi Lieber came to the United States from Stryj, Ukraine, in 1927, at the age of two with his family, and they settled on a farm in Pennsylvania. Young David (who speaks Yiddish, English, and Hebrew, and can read German, French, Latin, and Greek) was raised in an Orthodox home and decided in high school that the rabbinate called him. He graduated *magna cum laude* from the College of the City of New York in 1944, concurrently receiving a bachelor's degree from JTS.

After earning a master's degree from Columbia in 1947, he was ordained a rabbi in 1948 through JTS, studying under such luminaries as Saul Lieberman, H. L. Ginsberg, and Mordecai Kaplan. When they received an invitation from Congregation Sinai in 1950, the Liebers decided to try their luck out West. He received his doctorate in Hebrew Literature from the Seminary in 1951.

Like his predecessor, Rabbi Lieber delivered sermons on alternating Friday nights, took responsibility for the Hebrew school and youth programs, and managed the *bichur cholim* program for the congregation. He, too, enjoyed a very close relationship with Rabbi Kohn, whom he viewed as "an extraordinary human being, with no airs about him. He looked like a bishop, but didn't act like one." As he did with Rabbi Pressman, Rabbi Kohn loved to chat with Rabbi Lieber during Shabbat services ... until Mr. Ed Hyman finally separated them!

According to Rabbi Lieber, one of the best things that he learned from Rabbi Kohn was that "you can be a rabbi without being stuffy." In addition, Rabbi Kohn helped him understand that one must never underestimate the intelligence of a congregation: "They may not be learned, but they are not unintelligent." This was extraordinary advice coming from a very highly educated intellect, and demonstrates how much he respected everyone, regardless of their level of formal education. It also is evidence of his own understanding that as a rabbi, he served at the pleasure of his congregants.

Praying for Relief

One thing that was increasingly unclear during 1951 was the escalating conflict in the Korean peninsula. The United States began to send troops into the region and, only a year after he arrived, Rabbi Lieber left Sinai for two years to serve as a chaplain in the Air Force. Rabbi Kohn once again had to assume total responsibility for ministering to a large congregation, but he enthusiastically supported his young associate's detour since the senior rabbi himself had helped inaugurate the Jewish chaplaincy program in Europe during World War I. Still, he missed him greatly, and copies of many of Rabbi Kohn's letters to Rabbi Lieber (found in the archives) imply a warm and caring relationship.

Many changes started brewing during Rabbi Lieber's absence—changes that would affect not only the course of Congregation Sinai, but, ultimately, the young rabbi's career, as well. The Sinai school, originally set up in Beverly Hills as a stopgap measure to retain younger members by providing education for their children, had proved so successful that the

University of Judaism
WEST COAST BRANCH

The Jewish Theological Seminary of America, in California

612 South Ardmore Avenue • Los Angeles 5, California • DUnkirk 8-4155

June 3, 1953

BOARD OF GOVERNORS

Justin G. Turner
Chairman

Jacob Alkow
Mrs. Bertram Allenberg
David Bassan
Ely Elias
Mrs. Philip Dworsky
Julius Fligelman
Aaron Gordon
Max Holtzman
Peter M. Kahn, Jr.
Dr. David Klein
Meyer Krakowski
Cyrus Levinthal
Mrs. Albert E. Marks
Abe Morantz
Harry Rotblatt
Dr. Nathan S. Saltzman
Dr. Philip L. Seman
Theodore Strimling
Harold Wilkenfeld
Mrs. James Zofness

EX-OFFICIO

Dr. Samuel Dinin
Dr. Jacob Kohn
Mrs. Irwin A. Reiss

COMMITTEE CHAIRMEN

Dr. Philip L. Seman
Youth and Adult Education
Mrs. Albert E. Marks
Women's Institute
Dr. Nathan S. Saltzman
Teacher's Institute and Graduate School
Mrs. Maurice Turner
Fine Arts

UJ letterhead showing original building

elders began to search in earnest for property for a new Sinai home.

This in itself caused controversy because many "old timers" did not want to build a third synagogue. They felt that if the younger people wanted to move away, they could build their own synagogue. There was nothing wrong with the current one.

Rabbi Kohn saw his congregation in crisis and wrote to Rabbi Lieber, asking him to return to Los Angeles immedi-

RABBI JACOB KOHN
SINAI TEMPLE
407 SO. NEW HAMPSHIRE
LOS ANGELES 5, CALIF.

May 31, 1951

Dear Member:

Please read the enclosed carefully. You know that in a sense, the University of Judaism is a child of Sinai. Your Rabbi has, from the beginning, taught on its faculty and acted as Dean of the Graduate School. Mr. Platt and Mr. Strimling and several of the members of our Board have taken a kaen interest in its development.

The Seminary, of which Rabbi Lieber and myself are alumni, depends upon our members to take the lead in rallying to the support of the University. At present, it is asking only that you enroll as an Associate Member through payment of Ten Dollars annually.

I hope that you will not find this contribution a burden, and that you will be glad to have a part in the maintenance of this fine institution.

With warmest good wishes, I remain

Devotedly yours,

Jacob Kohn

Rabbi Jacob Kohn

JK.ar
encl.

Letter to the congregation from Rabbi Kohn

ately upon his discharge. He implored him to forego a planned 2-week family vacation to New York in order to help enlist the support of younger members to build a new temple on the Westside. He didn't want his strong synagogue to splinter simply because of geographic dissonance. Rabbi Kohn also admitted that he was tired and that his workload laid heavily on him. Sadly, too, Mrs. Kohn had

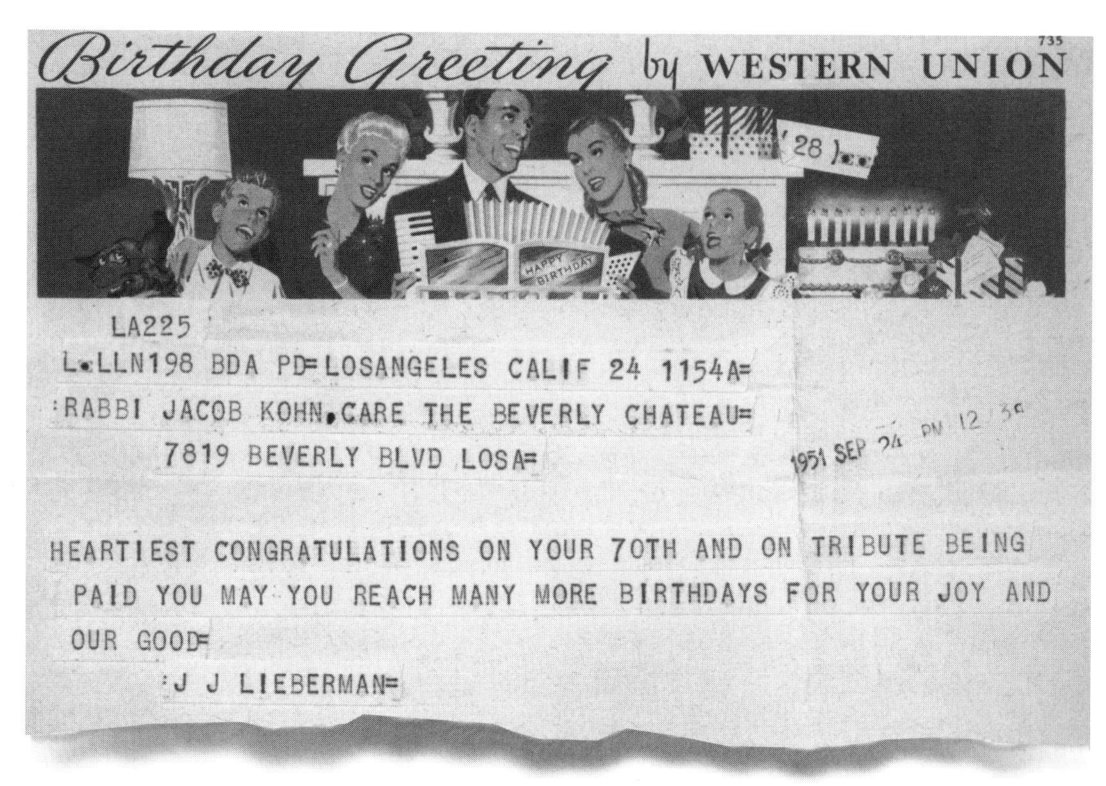
Birthday Greeting by WESTERN UNION

LA225
L.LLN198 BDA PD=LOSANGELES CALIF 24 1154A=
:RABBI JACOB KOHN, CARE THE BEVERLY CHATEAU=
7819 BEVERLY BLVD LOSA=

1951 SEP 24 PM 12 30

HEARTIEST CONGRATULATIONS ON YOUR 70TH AND ON TRIBUTE BEING PAID YOU MAY YOU REACH MANY MORE BIRTHDAYS FOR YOUR JOY AND OUR GOOD=
:J J LIEBERMAN=

Western Union Telegram

begun to suffer from poor health, and he wanted to be able to better attend to her increased needs.

Deeply concerned, Rabbi Lieber did return promptly and set about helping Rabbi Kohn achieve his goals. So admired was Rabbi Lieber, who had really been active at Sinai for only a year, that he was offered the pulpit upon Rabbi Kohn's impending retirement. At the same time, another temple also offered Rabbi Lieber the position of senior rabbi, precipitating a serious evaluation of his own future. He knew that building a new temple would require considerable time devoted exclusively to fundraising, something that would not allow him sufficient opportunity to pursue his heart's true desire: study. He concluded that he could not be a scholar and a pulpit rabbi at the same time, and respectfully declined both offers.

This forced the congregation to look quickly, yet carefully, for a senior rabbi to succeed Rabbi Kohn, who planned to continue serving the congregation and community as Sinai's rabbi emeritus. The temple needed someone who would adopt Rabbi Kohn's farsighted vision, but would adapt and enhance it by adding his own personal focus. It was a tough prescription to fill. Rabbi Israel Chodos proved a spectacular choice.

Rabbi Chodos Arrives at Sinai

At 6′3″, with an outgoing and ebullient nature, Rabbi Chodos was truly "larger than life." Even 40 years after his untimely demise, people still lovingly describe him this way. Born in Vilna (Lithuania) on November 22, 1905, young Israel came to the United States with his parents at the age of three. He received a primary education in public schools, graduated from Johns Hopkins University, took additional classes at Harvard, and was ordained from JTS with only eight other students. At the time they moved to Los Angeles, his wife, Judith, was in the process of obtaining a master's degree in English at the University of Oklahoma, which she completed at UCLA.

Prior to his tenure at Sinai, Rabbi Chodos held pulpits in White Plains, New York; Worcester, Massachusetts; and Indianapolis. For the immediate preceding seven years, he served as rabbi at Congregation Emanuel in Oklahoma City, where he was greatly loved. That synagogue doubled in size while he was there,

Golden Jubilee: Sophie Urstein, Jacob Deutch, Rabbi Kohn, Cantor Carl Urstein, Beverly Hills Hotel, December 9, 1956

necessitating the construction of a new temple, which he oversaw.

Rabbi and Mrs. Chodos had four sons: Hillel, Gabriel, Rafael, and Daniel. When the temple later moved to Westwood, the family moved to a house a few blocks away from the synagogue, and then they purchased a home at 818 S. Beverly Glen Boulevard, which still stands. Like the rabbi himself, the house is large and gracious, and congregants were always welcome.

According to the *Sinai Temple Bulletin* of March 3, 1955, which included a brief biography of the 49-year-old cleric, in Oklahoma he "lectured frequently to other groups and appeared on a weekly TV show, 'Your Bible,' in which he, a Catholic priest and a Protestant minister answered questions on the Bible. The rabbi also participated in another TV show, 'Our Better Shelves,' which dealt with great literature." The new rabbi could read Hebrew, Greek, Latin, German, French, Spanish, and Yiddish in addition to English, which gave him a tremendous command of language and literature that soon became apparent through his powerful sermons, filled with flowery phrasing and numerous literary references.

Rabbi Kohn and Theodore Strimling

Rabbi Kohn Retires

Rabbi Kohn officially retired after 25 years of devoted and inspired leadership. The temple honored him with numerous events and celebrations, including a gala dinner that also marked his 75th birthday. Best of all, he wasn't really leaving, merely transitioning in status, but not stature. And with Rabbi Chodos formally installed and enthusiastically embraced by the congregants, the temple seemed ready to begin the next phase of its journey. Like the United States itself, the motto of expansion seemed to be "Westward, ho!"

Future home of Sinai Temple: (left to right) Mrs. Ed Hyman, Harriet White, Lucille Waldman, Ozzie Goren, Franklin Benson, Ed Hyman

Chapter Eight

Westwood or Wither

As the temple developed, the years between 1953 and 1960 were a whirlwind of activity as well as conflict. Nearly 50 years old, the congregation stood at a crossroad of change that would quickly determine its fate. Depending on its members' choices, Sinai either could propel itself forward and grow, or stagnate and potentially wither.

After the retirement of Rabbi Kohn and the arrival of Rabbi Chodos, some highlights of this period included the purchase of a cemetery and the decision to move west.

Rabbi Lieber, who had so ably assisted Rabbi Kohn, chose intellectual pursuits, and left Sinai in 1954 to pursue other opportunities. Since then, he has had an illustrious and inspirational career, making a tremendous, posi-

tive impact on Jewish life locally and internationally. He served as president of the University of Judaism (UJ), where he is president emeritus today, as well as the Skovron Distinguished Service Professor of Literature and Thought. He was international president of the Rabbinical Assembly, and editor-in-chief of the *Etz Hayim* Torah commentary currently used by Sinai Temple, where the Rabbi and his wife, Dr. Esther Lieber, still belong.

The timing of Rabbi Chodos's arrival in 1955 couldn't have been better. Rabbi Kohn was ready to cut back on his workload and Rabbi Chodos quickly worked himself into Sinai culture. Unlike some of his predecessors, he regularly attended board meetings, but managed to express his views without exerting undue influence or alienating people. Perhaps the greatest evidence of things to come was a comment he made at a board meeting on December 14, 1955. According to the minutes, "Dr. Chodos appealed for a sense of high vision and outlook, projecting that the new Sinai Temple would be a nationally famous citadel of Conservative Judaism, and that plans for it should not be considered as those of a neighborhood synagogue."

Rabbi Chodos not only bought into the Kohn vision for a great and glorious future, but he also had plenty of other ideas to contribute. He saw Sinai as a leader within the ranks of the Conservative movement, especially through its unique and strong affiliation with the UJ.

Sinai soon became an even stronger congregation due to the extraordinary efforts of a recently retired attorney who had just relocated to Los Angeles from Chicago. Matthew Berman (originally from Boston) had served as vice president of the prestigious Congregation Anshe Emet in Chicago and was keen to continue his work advancing Conservative Judaism on the West Coast. In 1951, Mr. Berman wrote a letter to Simon Greenberg, head of the Jewish Theological Seminary, asking for information about forming a conservative synagogue in town.

Rabbi Greenberg responded by directing him to Harold Easton, a Sinai member who also was president of United Synagogue, as well as to Rabbi Kohn, who also was president of the Rabbinical Assembly of Southern California. In their roles outside of Sinai, both men had an obligation to help him in his quest. It is unclear why Mr. Berman initially considered forming a new congregation that would seemingly compete with Sinai: what is certain is that he ultimately joined Sinai, becoming a respected and popular member.

To Move or Not to Move

The greatest dilemma Sinai faced was whether or not to relocate to West Los Angeles. Rabbi Chodos's enthusiasm and dynamic personality worked well to help persuade congregants that the westward shift was not only necessary, but also was beneficial. A survey taken at the time showed that over 85 percent of the congregation supported the move.

Rabbi Chodos was already an old hand at building synagogues—he had just done the same thing in his Oklahoma community. Matthew Berman became a key ally of Rabbi Chodos when it came to implementing the move and building a new structure. He was a refined gentleman who performed like a bulldozer: he was dependable, focused, and just plain unstoppable when his heart was in a project. His heart was in this.

The situation played out like a ping pong match over the next several years—looking for suitable property, making offers and withdrawing them, making new offers, and considering how to physically and financially orchestrate such a monumental move. All the while, the Board of Directors remained fixed and focused on keeping the existing congregation afloat and vibrant. Then, as now, recruiting and retaining the younger generation was key.

Rabbi Speaks

The life of a Rabbi in an ever unfolding community and a vigorous, expanding Congregation such as ours, is filled with tremendous challenge. There is preaching and teaching. There is study and contemplation which are required to replenish the reservoirs of knowledge. There is the harrowing regimen dictated by the demands of a thousand administrative details which attend the effective execution of a ramified program of religious, educational, recreational and social activities.

Dr. Israel Chodos

But the greatest challenge of all, it seems to me, is the one which flows from an earnest desire on the part of the Rabbi to make himself a real influence in the personal lives of the members of his Congregation. A Rabbi achieves most when he earns the name of friend, not only mentor.

Your Rabbis at Sinai want most to become your personal friends. We want to share your happiness. We want to be with you at the moments of grief, God forbid. We want to rejoice in your triumphs. We want to be helpful in the personal problems that may involve you or your children. We try very hard to overcome the barrier of the impersonal which is, perhaps, the saddest characteristic of such a large city such as ours.

I want every member of Sinai to feel free to call upon me for any way in which I can be helpful. The spiritual leaders of Sinai stand ready at any time to guide you in the unraveling of your personal problems.

The Rabbis of your Temple are blessed with many gifts, except the gift of prophecy. Come to us. Let us know what you are thinking about. Let us help you in your hour of need. Let us be glad with you in your moments of joy. Keep us informed. Help us, please, to sow the seeds of a long and ever ripening friendship.

—Dr. Israel Chodos

Growing Up "Sinai" and Adult Education

The 1950s were idyllic for American families and golden years at Sinai: the war was over long enough for a sense of normalcy to have returned. Dad worked hard to support the family; mom worked hard to make a beautiful home and make her family proud; and bar mitzvah was the highpoint of a young boy's

Sinai Temple Board Authorizes Escrow for Additional Wilshire Boulevard Property

(*Sinai Speaks*, December 16, 1957)

At a special meeting of the Board of Directors called by President Eugene M. Rosen on November 12, 1957, and chaired by Benjamin Platt at the invitation of the President, the Board of Directors of Sinai Temple took another historic step when it authorized the purchase of the land contiguous to the property we now own on Wilshire Boulevard and Holmby Avenue. With the acquisition of this additional property, the new Sinai Temple will be erected on the entire block on Wilshire Boulevard from the southwest corner of Beverly Glen Boulevard to Holmby Avenue and southward to a depth of 200 feet. The additional land will make possible a far more effective arrangement of the necessary facilities, and will solve the parking problem. It will also considerably reduce overall construction costs.

The New Sinai will be built on the most commanding site on the West Coast. It will be a source of pride to every member of Sinai, to every member of the Jewish faith, and to the Los Angeles general community.

Jewish education, affirming his membership in the Jewish community.

In the early 1950s, the Conservative movement ratified bat mitzvah as a formal rite of passage for girls, but until then, confirmation was the crowning moment for Jewish girls before college and/or marriage. Congregation Sinai's first bat mitzvah took place not long after, opening the door for equal recognition and equal responsibilities for girls and women who wanted it.

Rabbi Herbert Teitelbaum joined the staff of Congregation Sinai as an associate rabbi at the age of 29, and his primary role was to supervise the schools. He was an outstanding education director and the first to recognize that Sinai needed a full-time professional dedicated to overseeing its expanding schools and programs. Rabbi Teitelbaum set the stage for a succession of noteworthy rabbis who became education directors over the next 20 years, leading the schools in their pursuit of excellence. These men included Julian White, Dan Merritt, Paul Dubin, and Paul Schneider.

But not all the directors were rabbis. One such extraordinary leader was Dr. Julius Lesner. A highly respected prin-

Rabbi Teitelbaum, Shirley Kirsch, Cantor Urstein and students.

cipal and administrator in the Los Angeles Unified School District, Dr. Lesner joined Sinai in 1955 when it was at 4th and New Hampshire. His greatest impact occurred between 1960 and 1985. He used all of his experience as a public school educator and administrator to guide Sinai toward hiring and training an outstanding educational staff and established stimulating, accredited curricula for the schools' growing "baby boom" youngsters.

Fourth and New Hampshire buzzed with educational activities for all age groups. Not only did Sinai conduct daily services and run several schools, but the UJ also held many of its classes there since its own building wasn't adequate for the number of students enrolled. Then as now, the UJ offered a wealth of classes in adult education for the entire community.

The community responded by attending in droves. With a national focus on edu-

cation made popular through the GI Bill, men and women who otherwise might not have had the chance to receive a college education flocked to centers of higher learning. Jewish adults, especially, took great advantage of myriad adult education opportunities, probably stemming from an already present cultural emphasis on learning.

Rabbi Chodos loved teaching, with the idea of expanding the mind and enriching the spirit. "Chats with Chodos," or "Sunday Chats," was perhaps his best known and most loved class, offered while the children were in Sunday school. (It also generated a handsome profit.) The temple owns fourteen recorded audiotapes of these classes, and they should be of great interest to historians.

Sinai's social programs—meaning, anything that brought folks together—grew in variety and increased in frequency. Typically, they were organized under the auspices of the Men's Club and Sisterhood, which enjoyed a resurgence in popularity as members gathered for picnics, banquets, and countless other activities. Among the most memorable were the plays and musicals mounted with the help of synagogue members who worked in the entertainment industry—or wished they did!

The Sinai Young People's League also proved quite popular. In 1955, according to *Sinai Speaks*, it held an open meeting devoted to the intricacies and enjoyment of the new medium: hi-fi. Today's equivalent might be USY holding a meeting to explain social and community networking using wireless digital media.

Cantor Carl Urstein and Music at Sinai

The one element of continuity that sustained the congregation throughout history was music, truly a Sinai hallmark. Cantor Carl Urstein and his wife, Sophie, joined the temple in 1947. The temple found a real treasure in this gentle man, someone who could convey the spirituality of the service through his voice. Cantor Urstein delighted everyone with his knowledge of Jewish liturgical song and sound and his skill in sharing a centuries-old heritage.

In liner notes to the 1966 phonograph record "Sabbath Music at Sinai," Mrs. Urstein—as charming as her husband—wrote comprehensive biographical notes worth quoting:

> *A sixth-generation Israeli of Chasidic ancestry, Cantor Urstein ... was acclaimed a child prodigy. ... he was boy soloist in the choir of the ancient Hurvah Synagogue of Jerusalem ... he won a scholarship to the Conservatory of Vienna, from which he was graduated as a "Bel Canto" singer of artistic rank. After having toured Europe and the Middle East in concerts of classic and*

liturgic music, he came to America where he was engaged as Cantor of the Anshe Emet Synagogue, one of the largest Conservative temples in Chicago.

In Chicago, Cantor Urstein won ... an enviable reputation as an outstanding Cantor and artist. No gala event of Jewish interest in the city was executed without his [participation], whether at a mass rally at the Chicago Stadium, Civic Opera or Orchestra Hall. Not only in the liturgical field has Cantor Urstein made an impress[ion], but he has also been acclaimed by the critics of the American and Jewish press as a genuine interpreter and composer par excellence of the songs of his native country. He became known in the West as the foremost living exponent of the Hebrew song as well as the Yiddish, Yemenite, Arabic and other oriental melodies.

ATTENDING FUNERAL Paying final respects to Bert Allenberg, Hollywood talent agent, are Danny Kaye, Edward G. Robinson, Buddy Adler, Joel McCrea, Frank Sinatra, Leo Durocher, Rabbi Israel Chodos, Frank Capra, Stewart Granger, Glenn Ford, Spencer Tracy, Abe Lastfogel, Sol Siegel, Sam Briskin, Ben Thau, Fred Zinnemann, Benjamin Dwoskin, Robert Woodburn, funeral director. Picture was taken as casket was placed in hearse, foreground, at entrance of Sinai Temple after the service. Many other stars of motion pictures were present at the funeral. (Times photo)

In 1947, Mr. Ben Platt, then president of Sinai Temple, attended one of Cantor Urstein's concerts and was so impressed that he invited him to become Cantor of Sinai, [where he has also served as] Music Director. Much of the music chanted at Sinai's services has been composed by the Cantor, who has attained pre-eminence in the community as a leading Cantor and noted composer of liturgical music. His appearance at the Hollywood Bowl in 1947 marked the first time that Hebrew music was orchestrated and sung there.

Mount Sinai Memorial Park

Mount Sinai Memorial Park (MSMP) originated in the early 1950s as the Jewish section of Forest Lawn Memorial Park, created by Hubert Eaton, who believed burial grounds should be a place of grandeur and inspiration, a place of contemplation *for the living* to keep alive the memories of those who have passed on—a place where one could celebrate the beauty of life and the lives of people resting there. MSMP in Hollywood comprises 82 rolling acres in the Hollywood Hills just across from Burbank. The entrance gate at the Park reads *"Beit HaChaim—House of Life."*

The first interment at Mount Sinai was in September 1953. At first, only single side-by-side interment spaces were provided, but in relatively short order, wall crypts and other kinds of property were constructed.

Sinai Temple's first formal contact with Mount Sinai evolved from the "reservation" in 1954 of a section of property for sale to temple members, an arrangement that benefited both the temple and Mount Sinai. Ben Dwoskin, a Sinai member who was then an employee of Forest Lawn, worked out the arrangement with Matthew Berman and Harold Easton, representing Sinai Temple.

Mr. Dwoskin became a member of the management team that began to oversee, on behalf of Forest Lawn, the management of MSMP. These people gradually became knowledgeable about the highly regulated burial business and worked hard to ensure that the Park conformed to highly prescribed Judaic, as well as state and

MSMP, Gardens of Shemot, features this beautiful mosaic floor.

Groundbreaking: Harold Easton at podium, June 14, 1959.

local, burial standards. They began to make MSMP a reliable and attractive interment option for the entire Los Angeles Jewish community.

In May 1958, MSMP broke ground for the construction of an administration building, Mount Sinai Chapel and Mount Sinai mortuary. Builders carried soil here from Mount Zion in Israel to mix with ground at the memorial park, symbolically blending ancient tradition with the modern vibrancy of American Judaism.

In early 1963, Forest Lawn was approached to ascertain if it would be interested in selling Mount Sinai to Sinai Temple. Matthew Berman was appointed by the Sinai Temple Board to spearhead the negotiations. At the July 9, 1963 Board meeting, the Resolution approving the purchase of MSMP from Forest Lawn was unanimously adopted.

The purchase price was $9,750,000. In order to effectuate the purchase, Sinai needed to borrow $500,000 to cover both the down payment and operating funds. The Board approached Alfred Hart, a Sinai member and the founding president of City National Bank which had only opened that year! The bank required the congregation to have its members personally sign notes guaranteeing the loan.

Sinai needed 20 members to each commit to $25,000, but only a few could easily assume such a pledge. Some did actually mortgage their houses—jeopardizing their own families' security—to help secure a proper Jewish burial place for the future. Fortunately, none of the original guarantors suffered any sort of personal loss as a result of undertaking this financial obligation.

The escrow for the purchase of Mount Sinai Memorial Park closed on

March 2, 1964. Temple financiers estimated it would take fifteen years to pay back the money they borrowed to achieve this, but to everyone's amazement, it took just over ten! This was because the MSMP management emphasized what was at that time a very innovative concept: pre-need purchase. So many people understood the importance and value of planning in advance that they purchased burial plots not only for themselves, but also for their children and sometimes *even their children's future spouses.*

Throughout the 50+ years, MSMP has made improvements to its operation by increasing available services and upgrading its facilities, transforming it into one of the most beautiful and admired memorial parks in the country. It has steadily built out additional parcels of its property turning them into tasteful and dignified gardens and crypts—under the expert guidance and supervision of Robert Levonian, one of the country's leading designers of memorial parks.

MSMP has installed beautiful art created by renowned artists throughout the property, including an extraordinary mosaic mural that is 145 feet long and three stories high that commemorates the history of the Jews in America, from their landing in New Amsterdam in 1654 to their westward expansion to California.

As of this writing in 2006, about 75,000 people are buried at MSMP in Hollywood. It is estimated that this property can continue to accommodate the community for about another 50 years.

Once Sinai Temple bought MSMP, it created a brand-new cemetery management committee (CMC) to govern the Park. This committee, an autonomous arm of the temple's board, was comprised, principally, of past presidents of the temple. The appointment to the CMC carries tremendous prestige and enormous responsibility, and has been, so far, a lifetime appointment for those asked to serve.

MSMP was originally organized as an endowed cemetery with funds going to an irrevocable endowment fund for the cemetery's upkeep. Currently an amount equal to 15% of the purchase price of cemetery property is placed in the fund.

MSMP is a huge operation and employs almost 150 employees, from executives, secretaries, and floral designers to consolation counselors, gravediggers, and security guards. Each person there performs a vital service. Rain or shine, everyone from the front office to the grounds crew always shows up.

In the early 1990s, the Cemetery Management Committee, first under the chairmanship of Herman Platt and then Dan Merritt, commenced studies projecting the eventual sell-out of all available property at Mount Sinai Hollywood Hills. These studies culminated in the purchase of some 360 acres of land in Simi Valley in 1996, 180 of which are designated for cemetery use and the creation of Mount Sinai Simi, which has been in operation since the late 1990s.

When MSMP opened, the least expensive plot available cost $75; today, of course, they cost much more. MSMP will never turn away an indigent Jewish family if the management is aware of their plight. Extreme financial hardship will not preclude a Jewish person from receiving a Jewish funeral and burial, with dignity, for all concerned.

Similarly, MSMP will never charge a family that loses a child under the age of 13, regardless of their financial standing. The CMC believes even the wealthiest family is impoverished upon the death of a child, and it is not fitting to charge for what is only decent.

Jewish funerals can be costly because of the many specialized services associated with Jewish burial. Jewish law requires some of them; civil law dictates others. As a provider to Orthodox families, MSMP strictly complies with *halacha* and upholds the highest standards. For example, *tehara*, the ritual washing of the body, is very specific and must be performed exactly. Because men are prohibited from handling women's bodies, MSMP employs two complete full-time *tahara* staffs, all of whom are Jewish.

Many people confuse *halacha* with Jewish practice, which can vary depending on whether a family is Ashkenazi, Sephardic, from Poland, or from Tunisia.

For instance, guarding the body with *shomrim* (watchmen) until it is interred is an ancient tradition that comes from needing to protect deceased loved ones from theft or harm. Today, in a modern 24/7 mortuary such as MSMP's, bodies are not unattended or left vulnerable. But people maintain this age-old practice because it makes them feel they are properly honoring the dead. The recitation of psalms is also not law, but custom.

There is nothing scripturally or legally that prohibits aboveground burial. Abraham buried Sarah in a cave; Rachael was buried in one, too. MSMP has aboveground crypts, and even kosher ones surrounded by earth.

Cremation, however, is a different matter. Each denomination of Judaism regards it differently, with assessments of its propriety ranging from absolutely forbidden (Orthodox) to acceptable (Reform). MSMP does not perform cremations at its mortuary, but it will allow cremated remains to be interred in the park.

MSMP serves the entire community; therefore, it supports the entire community in return. It makes major grants and allocations to help Jewish community services, schools, and synagogues throughout Southern California. It also has a remarkable Judaica collection available for public viewing. Conceived and started by Forest Lawn when it originally owned Mount Sinai, it consists of important artifacts bought in Israel and from sources across the United States.

When MSMP acquired the Park in 1964, Mr. Dwoskin—who planted the original seed for the Forest Lawn/Sinai Temple affiliation and became MSMP's founding general manager—took care to maintain the collection under his own watchful eye and nurture it, thanks to generous donations from the local Southern California community. In its entire history, the Park has had only two other general managers: Arnold Saltzman and currently Leonard Lawrence.

While there, Mr. Dwoskin also created an extraordinary group of scrapbooks that chronicle the history of the Park, Congregation Sinai, and Jewish leaders and dignitaries of the day. By preserving the past, he has assured that the history of the Park will be remembered with the same dignity it affords those who are buried there.

In 1955, one year after Sinai designated MSMP as its congregational cemetery, the temple sadly gathered there to bid farewell to its dear *rebbitzen* Augusta Kohn, who died after several years of declining health. Rabbi Simon Greenberg once said of her, "I know no person who is so universally loved and admired as she is." Her loss touched the entire community, and Congregation Sinai's Sisterhood commissioned a portrait of Mrs. Kohn, which they donated to the UJ in her memory.

Moving On

The benefit of having a congregational cemetery, however, would be of little consequence if the congregation itself ceased to exist. By 1956, and for the second time in its history, Congregation Sinai had to decide whether or not to move, and if so, where and how. Survival depended on making wise choices.

Its 4th and New Hampshire facility was bursting at the seams, proof of the synagogue's popularity. There was little room to accommodate newcomers who wanted to join. Yet, of its existing membership, the more successful families of longstanding started leaving in droves—moving west into the tony Westwood, Beverly Hills, and Brentwood neighborhoods. While the space these "defections" created would create room for new members at 4th and New Hampshire, it also signified that the core constituency might abandon the temple for geographic gratification.

Who should the temple aim to please? It was a serious dilemma for the board, Rabbi Chodos, Rabbi Emeritus Kohn, and everyone who loved Sinai.

If the temple were to move, Rabbi Chodos wanted a synagogue with a main sanctuary that could house at least 800 people, provide ample parking, and expand its seating to accommodate High Holiday crowds. Wherever such a temple would be built would require considerable space. Finding it on the Westside would be a challenge.

Nearly a decade earlier, in the late 1940s, Assistant Rabbi Jack Pressman had already started scouting properties in West Los Angeles that might be suitable for the westward-minded congregation. Rabbi Lieber engaged in a similar search in 1954, and found one at Sunset and Sepulveda, where the Luxe Hotel stands today. Initially, Sinai and the UJ considered partnering there to build a multipurpose facility that would serve both the temple and the university.

While both organizations would have derived significant benefit from such a union, the UJ reconsidered and withdrew from the venture. Sinai wasn't prepared to move forward alone at that site and resold it in hopes of finding something more appropriate. Its real estate hunt continued for nearly a decade, with alternate sites chosen and offers made, rescinded, or rejected. Opportunities slipped away while West Los Angeles rapidly developed and large affordable tracts of land dwindled.

The city block bounded by Wilshire Boulevard on the north, Ashton on the south, Beverly Glen on the east, and Holmby on the west, was situated at the pinnacle of prestigious Wilshire Boulevard ... at the highest point along its downtown–to–Santa Monica traverse. The four corners of the block had different owners and, in time, each section would become increasingly important for the temple's future. In the early 1950s, the northwest corner at Wilshire and Holmby was for sale.

Sinai saw its opportunity and immediately began determining how to afford it. The property had almost double the square footage of 4th and New Hampshire. With personal pledges obtained from a hastily organized building fund drive, plus a bank loan—and after successfully convincing the suddenly reluctant seller that she should consummate the deal—Sinai had its equivalent of a new mountaintop location by 1956. Nothing could be more fitting for the West Coast's flagship Conservative congregation.

What should have been a fairly straightforward enterprise of developing

and building out the property turned into one of the most convoluted experiences that, in some ways, made it completely typical for Sinai. Not surprisingly, Rabbi Chodos took an enormous interest in the project. Matthew Berman worked side by side with him. In only a few years, Mr. Berman had earned the respect of the board, which gave him numerous positions of increasing responsibility. Perhaps the board's highest tribute to this relative newcomer was entrusting him with the monumental task of overseeing construction of the new temple. Two years into the process, the congregation elected him president.

Getting Off to a Shaky Start

If the Rabbi was the "idea man," Mr. Berman can be described as "the muscle." When the temple finally found the site at Wilshire and Holmby, they turned to Sidney Eisenshtat with the notion that an important building needed an important architect: he was the "artist" to execute their vision. The men knew of Mr. Eisenshtat from several years before when the UJ hired him as its consultant for the property purchased in concert with Sinai Temple at Sunset and Sepulveda.

Sidney Eisenshtat, A.I.A., had a stellar professional reputation nationally, both in the secular and Jewish communities. He had already designed several important synagogues around the country, including Temple Emmanuel in Beverly Hills. Mr. Eisenshtat lived in Los Angeles and was well known locally for his excellent character. An Orthodox Jew, he was deeply committed to education and held leadership roles in many groups in the city, including the Bureau of Jewish Education. He also taught and studied Torah for his entire life, earning the love and admiration of those fortunate enough to have known him. When Mr. Eisenshtat died at the age of 92 in February 2005, no fewer than five rabbis eulogized him at his funeral attended by hundreds of friends and associates.

The architect collaborated with Rabbi Chodos and Mr. Berman for a very long time before the job was actually awarded to him. It was a time, especially among Jews, when business was conducted on a handshake. Nevertheless, due to a confluence of confusing circumstances, the project stopped progressing smoothly before it was officially awarded to anyone. The temple almost pulled the job from Sidney Eisenshtat and Associates in favor of another architectural firm ... even though Mr. Eisenshtat had already consulted for nearly two years and completed preliminary drawings everyone admired. Fortunately, the misunderstanding was resolved, but the incident foreshadowed future troubles.

Eventually the temple awarded Mr. Eisenshtat the job. Rabbi Chodos was a creative artist himself and committed to this architect ethically and morally. Mr. Eisenshtat was a strong-willed designer who was true to his vision and invested his own love of Judaism and profound Talmudic insight into every synagogue he helped design. And Mr. Berman knew how to communicate both men's passion to the more nuts-and-bolts board. He encouraged the architect to keep moving forward in spite of frequent setbacks, confident he could prevail over any conflict with the board. Together, they made a powerful trio.

Mr. Eisenshtat faced many challenges while erecting the new temple. He used an open bidding process—on every job—to choose his general contractor. He preselected, with client approval, a small group of excellent contractors, all of whom considered capable of doing the job. Mr. Eisenshtat would issue identical specifications, and then automatically award the job to the lowest bidder.

Since contractors knew he showed no favoritism except to a low bottom line, they generated honest bids, knowing better than to pad their budgets since it could cost them the job. Sinai undermined Mr. Eisenshtat by rejecting the lowest bidder and picking a more expensive contender. He nearly walked off the job, stunned that a temple would so blatantly disregard his work ethic and compromise his professional reputation.

Once that had been patched up, the temple announced it was $150,000 short of the estimated costs to which it had committed itself ... but it still wanted the same building, with all the fancy bells and whistles. Architect and contractor agreed to give the temple a four-month grace period to find the money while preconstruction continued, but, at the end of that time, if it hadn't materialized, Sinai would have to make cutbacks. It is fair to say that many people's prayers were answered, and Sinai Temple was truly built on angels' wings.

Separately, during the development process, but before any construction had begun, the quadrant of land at Wilshire and Beverly Glen became available—or would be—if the temple could do two things: guarantee the asking price of nearly $500,000 ... and guarantee it *overnight!* Acquiring this property would give Sinai the entire frontage between Beverly Glen and Holmby. Twice as much prestige, not to mention twice the debt (if not more!).

An emergency executive board meeting was convened: the board agreed to guarantee the price and do so *immediately!* Raising $500,000 in 24 hours was no small feat, but the temple's bankers communicated clearly to the seller's agents that

the temple was sincere and prepared to go forward. But when the seller then insisted that the temple give *triple* proof of its bona fides, even Rabbi Chodos thought they might be biting off more than they could chew. So Sinai backed away.

"Build It and They Will Come"

The groundbreaking for the new temple took place on September 22, 1957. Rabbi Kohn, renowned for orating easily for hours, delivered a succinct, one-sentence remark to commemorate the occasion: "When you look up to the heavens, your feet will be on consecrated grounds." Rabbi Chodos followed with his own poetic comments, and people's hopes soared. Afterwards, Rabbi and Mrs. Chodos held a reception at their home for the entire congregation. Over the next three years, Wilshire Boulevard would witness the birth of a white structure that bore no resemblance to either of Sinai's previous homes, or much of anything else at the time.

Until the new sanctuary was completed in 1960, Sinai remained active at 4th and New Hampshire, although it also held Shabbat and holiday services in Westwood for the members who steadily had been relocating to the Westside in anticipation of the temple's full move. Rabbi Max Vorspan, the renowned historian, author, and teacher, conducted those services at the Westwood Community (today, United) Methodist Church with the musical assistance of Max Helfman, another superstar who all-too-briefly graced the Sinai "stage." Among his many outstanding career highlights, Mr. Helfman was a conductor of the People's Philharmonic Chorus of New York, music director of the Brandeis Youth Foundation, and a founder and dean of the School of Fine Arts at the UJ.

The elegant Methodist church on Wilshire Boulevard at Warner Avenue was a very good neighbor for many years while Sinai was in transition. Every day on the hour, when the church's signature bells pealed across Westwood, Sinai members were reminded of the harmonious history these two houses of worship shared. Those bells still ring hourly, and many Sinai members can still appreciate their sound when walking to *shul*.

What no one would ever see while walking (or driving) past Sinai was a gigantic stained glass mural created by the famous Marc Chagall. One of Chagall's most important collectors (a Catholic friend of a Sinai member) contacted the artist, who offered to create something unique, yet unquestionably affordable. Even 50 years ago, Chagall was an international sensation, whose dream-like works were owned by major museums around the world.

Rabbi Chodos, Mr. Berman, and Mr. Eisenshtat were so excited by the prospect that the architect happily redesigned the entire face of the synagogue to feature Chagall's art windows. Unfortunately, in a colossal misjudgment of its directors at the time, no one else beyond the "Temple Trio" thought having an original Chagall stained glass mural was important, so the Sinai-Chagall commission never happened.

Even without Marc Chagall or his windows, the new Sinai Temple on Wilshire Boulevard attracted world attention. The following review, reprinted from the *New York Times* (8/7/60), testified to its architectural beauty and spiritual grandeur:

> *The Conservative Sinai Temple, costing $3,500,000 is rising spectacularly from one full block on Wilshire Boulevard in this Los Angeles suburb. It is scheduled for completion in September.*
>
> *To the congregation's Rabbi, Israel Chodos, the Temple will be a "reflection of 4,000 years of Judaism, with an eye to the future."*
>
> *To the architect, Sidney Eisenshtat, "Sinai Temple will be a beautiful piece of sculpture in an island of apartment houses."*

The new sanctuary.

> *The edifice has an eighty-foot-high stained glass tower. Thirteen multi-colored pyramids—the number is a mystical symbol in Judaism—run the length of the façade.*

Disappearing Wall

Inside, the Temple is divided into the sanctuary and the community hall, separated by a wall 120 feet wide and thirty feet high. To accommodate the High Holy Days overflow attendance, the wall, at the push of a button, will move upward and be concealed in a specially-constructed ceiling.

The sanctuary is designed along radical lines. The Ark, which contains the Holy Scriptures, will reveal, when opened, a twenty-foot tapestry done by the Israeli artist, Yehoshua Kovarsky. Immediately behind the Ark is an eighty-foot high stained glass window, the only window in the sanctuary, composed of thousands of chipped and faceted pieces of glass set into a special matrix. All lighting and cooling units are concealed in the ceiling, thus making the lecterns and the Ark the focal centers.

The seating is arranged in chevron-shaped rows so that every worshipper has a view of the lecterns. Nine hundred and twenty-six persons can be seated and when the partition is raised, there are seats for more than 1,800.

Although Sinai Temple is the oldest Congregation in the Los Angeles area, the architecture is as new as tomorrow. "There is no need," says Rabbi Chodos quoting the architect, "to wear a celluloid collar in 1960."

He adds, "When finished, this new Temple will serve as a center of Jewish culture, art and music, besides its basic function as a House of Worship."

The Sinai Choir under the direction of Alfred Sendry: Keith Wyatt, Estelle Marlov, Dr. Sendry, Nancy Nash, Lee Winter

The Rabbi's words would soon prove true. In dramatic fashion, the venerable Sinai Temple—in perfect readiness for the 5721 High Holy Days—welcomed worshippers into its pristine new sanctuary for the first time at midnight, September 17,

1960, for Selichot services. Rabbi Chodos beamed as Cantor Urstein chanted ancient music that transcended time, and the Sinai Choir—under the direction of Dr. Alfred Sendry—joined the Cantor in glorious praise of God. With Rosh HaShana days away, a spirit of rebirth and a sense of possibility filled the air, and everyone at Sinai said a *shehechayanu* for the miracle at hand.

Rabbi Kohn prepares wedding documents.

Chapter Nine

Building for the Future

Looking like a 21st-century tent sheltering a 6,000-year-old heritage, the awe-inspiring new sanctuary took one's breath away upon walking inside and experiencing its modern, stark holiness. Mr. Eisenshtat and Rabbi Chodos succeeded in creating an enormous, sacred space that subtly, yet inescapably, focused attention toward the signature ark containing precious Torah scrolls. Opposite the ark, at the rear of the sanctuary, was the astonishing 64,000-pound wall that could silently rise and disappear into the ceiling to reveal an adjoining social hall designed in complete harmony with the sanctuary.

Understandably, not everyone liked what was there. Compared to the traditional, European majesty of the two previous sanctuaries—with their ornate stained glass windows,

G-20
Saturday—TIMES Proof • Comp. #104—
1-7-61
• Proofs to Bartlett

FOR SALE

AT LESS THAN 1/3 ITS VALUE

Beautiful Building Suitable
for any membership organization or
religious institution

Opportunity for a rare bargain. Sanctuary fully carpeted and completely furnished, seats 1376. 4 rooms off loge and lobby. Social hall seats 300, with small kitchen off stage. Dining hall seats 300, with full kitchen, check room, extra room. 5 offices and storage on 2nd floor. 13 closet storage rooms, Custodian apartment 2nd floor, rear. Sale price $400,000 (approximate value $1,250,000.) Courtesy to brokers. Phone BR. 2-6336 or GR. 4-1518.

LOCATED AT 3412 W. 4th St., Los Angeles 5

Fourth and New Hampshire for sale.

elegant chandeliers, and other highly decorative features—the new temple stood in profound visual contrast to conventional houses of worship. While heavenly to some, it felt cold and impersonal to others. Even today, nearly 50 years after its construction, the temple's style does not appeal to everyone. Many members resigned after the new building was completed.

Among them was a loud contingent of congregants who opposed the construction on principle: they felt it was not financially sound to take on new debt immediately after burning the mortgage. Others jumped ship because they had already constructed two Sinai temples. They felt outraged to be expected to contribute to a third building fund when there was nothing "wrong" with the current location ... except that young people weren't joining. Some "old timers" actually asserted that if young people wanted to move west, they should start their *own* congregation with their *own* money and not effectively plunder 4th and New Hampshire in terms of cash or clergy.

Finally, the temple lost another contingency: many elderly congregants that *couldn't* move west, and for them, the new Sinai was just too far away. Rabbi Kohn, too old to drive himself, submitted to being driven to *shul* on Shabbat by Dr. George Shecter and others.

More Building; More Money

The mass departure of embittered members in 1960 when the new building was finished left Sinai with only 475 members, down from a one-time high of nearly 600. Expenses outweighed income to the tune of nearly $10,000 a month, making the temple desperate for new members to help reverse the negative cash flow.

The temple began a marathon of entertainment-oriented fundraisers to raise money to cover expenses. Those who admired the new "White Wonder" on Wilshire began an active grassroots cam-

Installation of officers, 1964 reception.

paign to enlist friends and Westside residents to join.

Settling In

Madalyn Honig Sandler, Sinai's first bat mitzvah on December 5, 1959 (4 Kislev 5720), offers a sweeping summation of the transition into Westwood and the ensuing adjustment to the new synagogue:

> *Can you imagine what it felt like to attend Friday night services in a church [Westwood Methodist], attend religious school in a motel with little hearts on the doors [next door stood an old motel on property that Sinai bought shortly after purchasing the property for the sanctuary]. Upon termination of the motel's lease, Sinai planned to convert it into a temporary schoolhouse until a proper facility could be built as part of the second phase of the Wilshire/Beverly Glen development], experience Rabbi Kohn blessing the congregation with outstretched arms and fingers stretched in the configuration of the letter V... the awe of stepping into the new sanctuary for the first time, and amazement at an entire wall being lifted into the ceiling, and, of course, the first High Holy Day service before air conditioning was installed in the sanctuary (don't know if we would have made it through without the smelling salts).*

Rabbi Chodos and Rabbi Teitelbaum at the Ark.

She refers to one of the best anecdotes in the temple's history, concerning the first High Holiday services in the new sanctuary. The air conditioning had not yet been installed. As luck would have it, the temperature soared during the holidays that year. Rabbi Chodos encouraged all the beautifully attired men and women to remove their hats, gloves, coats, and ties in order not to faint from the heat. Many passed out anyway. Something had to be done.

Al Mayhew, the custodian at the time, understood the dire situation, luckily, and ran out to purchase heavy blocks of ice. Some of the most prominent men in the congregation helped him carry them up the back stairs to the top of the rising wall (which looked perfect and worked, but somehow was not totally finished). They perched the enormous ice blocks on the wall and frantically fanned them, forcing down the temperature. It was so hot that the ice didn't drip or melt, but simply evaporated.

Twenty-five up-and-coming members of the congregation met in the foyer. Allen Ziegler said, "The air conditioning will cost $25,000. I'm putting in $1,000. How about you? And you? And you?" No one could turn him down, and the money was raised in about 10 minutes. Soon after, the sanctuary had air conditioning.

Death in the Line of Duty

The times were conducive to giving more than 100 percent, both in terms of money and effort. As John F. Kennedy suggested in his 1960 inaugural address, "Ask not what your country can do for you—ask what you can do for your country."

JFK energized America like no one had since FDR. People believed in the power of the present and the promise of the future. Nothing seemed impossible, so raising funds for a second round of construction at Sinai didn't either. It offered Sinai-ites a challenge to make their synagogue a symbol of the very best of America, as well as a reflection of the Jewish people.

Wilshire and Beverly Glen consisted of the sanctuary and social hall, which took precedence over the school and administrative offices during construction. But decreased membership rolls hadn't reduced the number of school students, and the kids needed a suitable learning environment quickly. The next capital campaign began.

Leading the way was the effervescent Rabbi Chodos, to whom life seemed like an endless feast of spiritual, intellectual, and poetic delight. He loved public life as a rabbi, was delighted with the new sanctuary, and enthusiastic about building the rest of Mr. Eisenshtat's vision. The only thing that slowed down the rabbi was his decline in health over the previous months due to complications from diabetes diagnosed in his youth.

President Kennedy's assassination in November 1963 shook people's faith to the core. For the nation, it represented a loss of innocence from which it could never recover. Houses of worship around the world convened to pray for Kennedy's soul and to sustain the living, who turned to each other for comfort. Sinai was no exception.

About two months earlier, Rabbi Chodos had undergone a leg amputation. With his recovery barely underway, he insisted on returning to work part time after the assassination, getting around in a wheelchair. It would be difficult to say whether he came back to help Sinai recover, or whether he drew energy for his own recovery from the healing love of his congregants. Most likely, it was both.

One day, a very small child bluntly asked, "Rabbi, where is your leg?" All the adults in hearing distance flinched. But the rabbi didn't. Being a wise and kind man, he couldn't embarrass the youngster for asking a good question. In his inimitable style, with a twinkle in his eye, he replied, "I folded it up and tucked it in my pocket."

And then, only one month after President Kennedy died, Sinai's beloved Rabbi Chodos, just 58 years old, succumbed to his illness, reopening a gaping wound of grief. Congregants were heartbroken. They were deprived again of a leader they loved—a giant among men. And even though the rabbi didn't form close relationships with many members of Sinai—in an attempt to avoid any appearance of favoritism or partisanship—nearly everyone viewed him as a friend.

One Door Closes, Another Opens

With Rabbi Chodos's passing, Rabbi Kohn found himself again at the helm of the most important Conservative synagogue on the West Coast, only this time he was in his 80s. Thirty years earlier, when associate rabbis Pressman and Lieber left Sinai, the increased workload was tough on Rabbi Kohn. By 1964, it was clearly too much for the still-spry octogenarian to handle alone.

Fortunately, Rabbi Daniel Merritt, Sinai's director of education, picked up the slack and truly saved the day. He humbly and ably fulfilled the additional duties required of a pulpit rabbi. As a measure of appreciation, respect, and esteem, the board bestowed upon him the new title of Assistant Rabbi, with a lifetime membership.

Sinai Temple's Rabbi

Regular Virtues

The rabbi must be a good human being; a good pastor; a good preacher; a good administrator; a good organizer; a good educator; a good writer; a healthy young man (who was mature, but young enough to stay with Sinai for at least 20 years' service).

Special Virtues

He must be of sufficient stature to attract people to Sinai and make it the dominant temple in Los Angeles; have outstanding qualities to be considered the key person in the Los Angeles Rabbinate; be referred to publicly, by non-Jews, as the rabbi most representative of the Jewish community (he should be the "go to" rabbi quoted by papers and broadcast media). He must have the ability to attract scholars and teachers from UCLA, the UJ, and other institutions of learning (and be the rabbi invited to speak at those places, too); the ability to make Sinai the most dynamic congregation in America; and, he should be a man who can give us the preeminence as a congregation that Sinai has as a facility.

Sinai Temple needed a replacement for Rabbi Chodos. Most interesting in terms of the congregation's development, President Herman Platt, son of former president Ben Platt, did not simply announce to the board whom he had chosen to replace Rabbi Chodos ... as his father had done in selecting Rabbis Kohn, Pressman, Lieber, and even Chodos. Instead, he organized a search committee, writing a list of ideal qualities the synagogue sought in its next leader. Called "Sinai Temple's Rabbi—What His Virtues Should Be," the document enumerated "regular" and "special" virtues.

About Sinai Temple, Platt wrote:

> *There is no finer sanctuary anywhere and no better urban location. This alone gives Sinai stature. Sinai needs the spiritual leadership to make its potential come to fruition; must be able to work closely with the UJ and JTS; must be able to take advantage of this time in Sinai's history to thrust the congregation forward into the destiny that potentially has been available for years, but which has eluded it; must be a strong man.*
>
> *Sinai is a tough congregation to motivate. Hundreds, and even thousands of children will also be influenced by our choice because they will or will not be properly encouraged to grow up into the fine Jewish men and women we look for from Sinai.*

Rabbi Hillel Silverman

The search led them to a talented rabbi at Congregation Shearith Israel in Dallas, Texas, who nearly came to Los Angeles only a few years before. Rabbi Hillel Silverman had served Shearith Israel for almost ten years when he received an offer from Valley Beth Shalom in Encino, California. He accepted the offer because, among other reasons, he wanted to rear his children in a much larger and more Jewish environment than Dallas could provide at the time. But almost immediately, he rethought his decision and within days rescinded his acceptance, opting to stay in Dallas a while longer.

After Rabbi Chodos died, Allen Ziegler heard that Rabbi Silverman might be available, and he was among a small group of people that went to Dallas to observe him. The Silvermans' elder daughter became bat mitzvah that weekend, so they could easily witness the rabbi's full emotional range. When Rabbi Pressman learned that Rabbi Silverman was under consideration for the Sinai post, he immediately endorsed him.

During his candidacy, Rabbi Silverman disclosed the VBS incident to the board. Before Sinai offered him the position, it made overtures of goodwill to VBS to obtain the *shul*'s assurance of *shalom bait*. With it, and having done its due diligence, Sinai Temple chose Rabbi Hillel Silverman to lead it into the future.

In the summer of 1964, the Silvermans moved to Los Angeles. The rabbi's impressive knowledge of Torah, along with his natural warmth and charm, quickly proved adept at bringing the congregation together as it moved beyond mourning both its national and spiritual leaders. Within a few years, the rabbi and his wife joyfully announced the birth of a son, Jonathan, who would become a successful and popular actor.

Hillel Emanuel Silverman was born in 1924, the son of Rabbi Morris Silverman, author of the "Silverman Siddur" used in almost every Conservative congregation, and Althea O. Silverman, a highly spiritual woman who was also the sister of Sinai's *shammes*, Maurice Osber.

A 1945 *summa cum laude* graduate of Yale, Hillel Silverman served on the debate team. He also studied at Hebrew University in Jerusalem and became a member of the Haganah underground, fighting in the Arab-Israeli war. At JTS, his roommate, Jack Pressman, became his lifelong friend. Rabbi Silverman married an Israeli, Devora Halaban, and graduated from JTS with advanced degrees in Hebrew Literature (1949) and Hebrew Bible (1951).

The Silvermans' first daughter was born in 1951, and the rabbi and his family

traveled the world while he served as a chaplain in the U.S. Navy during the Korean War. Upon completion of his service, the family settled in Dallas, where a second daughter was born in 1959.

Rabbi Silverman was probably the greatest fundraiser on behalf of the temple among all the clergy in its history. He knew how to connect with people in large groups and, especially, one-on-one. He also was known for his outstanding work with youth: Sinai's youth groups flourished during his almost two-decade tenure.

And then there were his sermons. Rabbi Silverman was a real "old-time religion" preacher, working up a sweat while he passionately delivered oratory that drew the attention of Jewish Los Angeles. People outside Sinai came often to hear him, which benefitted the temple with increased membership. The charismatic rabbi also created joint programming with Camp Ramah, which at that time was headed by Rabbi Zvi Dershowitz.

Many temple members became highly active in the *shul* during this time. Doris Siegel, who would later become the temple's first female president, grew up at Sinai, and got her start by volunteering at the school after dropping off her children on Sunday mornings. She also worked in the office, but refused a salary. Mrs. Siegel became Rabbi Silverman's friend and right-hand person, gaining the knowledge and experience that would contribute to her lifelong commitment to Sinai Temple.

As Mrs. Siegel's star began to rise, Sylvia Tansey decided to "retire." A devoted and talented congregant, she single-handedly put together and shaped *Sinai Speaks* for nearly 20 years on a volunteer basis, turning it into the important newsletter it remains today, still retaining the look and style she instituted.

Sinai Speaks is an integral part of the temple, arriving monthly through the mail, heralding the latest events, *mitzvot*, *simchot*, and passings, and chronicling modern times through the rabbis' messages. Although some might take *Sinai Speaks* for granted, the board understands the time-consuming work required to produce it. When Mrs. Tansey stepped down, the board honored her for her years of fine work and dedication. Since then, several other talented volunteers have overseen the newsletter's regular publication.

A particular group of young men who became active at Sinai around this same time referred to themselves as the "Young Turks." They had bold ideas about running the temple—ideas in opposition to sitting leadership. They could be seen around the temple regularly, serving on committees, stirring up controversy or, sometimes, doing both. All these men would prove important in the temple's history: Aaron Fenton, William Friedland, Dr. Edward Kamenir, and Allen Ziegler. Each would go on to become a Sinai president—the very establishment they rebelled against.

Turbulent Times Surround the Temple

The 1960s brought civil rights to the forefront of national consciousness. Sinai Temple, in sync with the Conservative movement, took a strong position in favor of social change, encouraging members to remember religious doctrine that preached true brotherhood and to support public policy that endorsed equality among all people.

While racial unrest rocked the country, the Vietnam conflict escalated, too, with troops going overseas to fight a campaign not many understood and, over time, even fewer believed in. Conversations around dinner tables centered on drugs, the draft, draft dodging, Canada, grad school, and Conscientious Objector status. Concurrently, feminism took hold among young and young-minded women, and they began to define their own identity, rather than be defined by their fathers or through their husbands.

In times of political and social instability, people often turn toward their faith for solace and direction. Rabbi Silverman, with his reassuring voice and unbridled optimism, guided his congregants through the morass into the future. He focused their energies on Sinai's growth and on maintaining its role as premier Conservative synagogue of the West Coast.

Angels Among Us

As everyone knew, the construction of the sanctuary was only the first stage of Sinai's Westwood renaissance. Fundraising for the school building, administrative offices, and a chapel that the Ziegler family wanted to name in memory of their friend Augusta Kohn had started almost as soon as the sanctuary opened. Then, in July 1964, just before Rabbi Silverman arrived, another quadrant of the city block where Sinai stood (1225 S. Beverly Glen, at the corner of Ashton) came up for sale. Its owner offered it straightaway to the temple, knowing it could use the footage to build out, yet again, at some future time.

The price was very high. Sinai couldn't really afford it, but it couldn't afford to let someone else buy it because this could seriously jeopardize the temple's future if it wanted or needed to expand again later. For two months, buyer and seller negotiated, and then it was announced that "a member" had purchased

Groundbreaking Phase II construction — 1967

it privately and would hold it to sell to the temple at cost ... whenever the temple was ready and able to afford it. No one knew who it was. Years later, this member held true to his word. Not surprisingly, it was Allen Ziegler.

Mr. Ziegler had, by then, become one of Sinai's most influential members. He was a well-liked man, who gave of his time and of himself. He was indisputably committed to the growth of Sinai in all possible ways and brought a personal joy to everything he did there.

In 1964, he was elected president of the congregation but, unfortunately, health issues required his stepping down early. All the same, he didn't disappear. He still commanded tremendous respect, playing an ongoing and pivotal part in Sinai's development. Like the venerable Ben Platt, he became the "go to" person when serious questions arose.

Times and Tastes Change

One of those serious questions concerned hiring an architect to build Phase II. Architect Sidney Eisenshtat had long since drafted plans for the "expansion," as it were, since it was part of his comprehensive original vision for the new Sinai Temple. All concerned knew the construction must occur in stages since the entire cost all at once would be prohibitive.

The second phase of the project was, in essence, completion of the total design. Although Sinai did not officially commit to Mr. Eisenshtat up front, for what would be the second portion of the construction, the job was his by implication all along (at least in the minds of Rabbi Chodos and Mr. Berman), barring some disaster during Phase I.

The expansion incorporated an extension of the entranceway (including more triangular-shaped stained glass windows) eastward toward the motel, which would be razed. Upon completion of Phase II, Sinai would appear to stretch seamlessly along Wilshire Boulevard from Beverly Glen to Holmby. It would be the grandest, most glorious house of worship—a beacon of virtue at the top of the hill; something "fitting" in the opinion of the late Rabbi Chodos, who consistently envisioned Sinai on a large and impressive scale.

The only problem was that Rabbi Chodos was gone and, without him, Matthew Berman, president during Phase I, no longer had an ally pushing the project forward. He and Rabbi Chodos were the two people in the synagogue best able to articulate Mr. Eisenshtat's complete vision to the board. But during the elapsed time from the inception of the project to its current state, Mr. Berman's term had ended, and the board had changed, leaving the independent-minded, award-winning architect without the *carte blanche* support he once enjoyed.

The board felt they couldn't control Mr. Eisenshtat in terms of costs and accountability. (Whether an accurate assessment or not, it was the board's stated impression.) Heated discussion took place among the building committee members as they sought a different architect.

The first phase of construction *had* been very expensive, with Rabbi Chodos's enthusiasm for high-tech enhancements such as specially equipped *bimah* chairs. Each one had a built-in microphone and speaker system permitting the rabbi to chat with anyone sitting anywhere on the *bimah*. He also could communicate with front-door ushers, who told him who arrived, along with other pertinent information.

These bells and whistles were preposterously expensive in 1959; to remain on budget, implementing them would have necessitated eliminating important architectural design elements, and that would have seriously compromised the overall project. A true visionary artist, Mr. Eisenshtat fought hard for what he believed was essential, but he knew Rabbi Chodos wouldn't sacrifice his chairs or several other "wish-list" items. Because the architect was equally passionate about making Sinai a stunning architectural gem and knew he couldn't do without certain stylistic features, Mr. Eisenshtat personally absorbed many project costs, unbeknownst to anyone until much, much later.

Documents, including board minutes and interviews, corroborate that Mr.

Phase II: Construction of the school and administrative offices, June 1967.

Eisenshtat was told that if he wanted to be considered for the next phase of work, he would have to submit to an interview, like all candidates. In response, he told the committee that the sanctuary, and everything else he built so far, *were* his "interview" and that should suffice. The board wrongly assumed this to mean he wasn't interested—or it was a convenient reason not to consider someone they didn't unanimously agree upon—and they never interviewed him.

Numerous architects refused the invitation to interview out of respect for their colleague, who essentially had been "promised" the entire job ten years earlier, knowing he had designed the second stage as an organic part of the creative whole. Many years later, Sidney Eisenshtat offered his own assessment about the loss of this commission: "The fact that we did not do the second part of Sinai was one of the tragedies—professional tragedies—of my life."

The Wizard of Wilshire: Dr. Edward Kamenir

Ultimately, the temple awarded the job to Howard Frank, who completed the work on time and on budget, and who delivered a beautiful building that incorporated several of Mr. Eisenshtat's ideas.

Overseeing Mr. Frank's work was one of Sinai's "Young Turks," Dr. Edward Kamenir. He and his wife, Charlotte, moved to Los Angeles from Chicago in the mid-1950s, and Harriet White (a future president of Sisterhood) recruited them to join the temple. The Kamenirs became active in youth programming and recruiting and retaining new, younger members through a variety of initiatives. When Sinai first needed to find land to move west from 4th and New Hampshire, Dr. Kamenir had been indispensable in helping to find it.

A dentist by formal training, Dr. Kamenir has a wide range of interests spanning everything from art to science to business as well as a desire to get involved with real estate and development. While continuing to practice dentistry *yet again*, he decided nearly 50 years before to earn an additional license as a building/general contractor. In 1974, he returned to school to earn a law degree at night while still pursuing all his other interests.

When Sinai began its construction of the chapel, school, and offices, it made perfect sense for Henry Traub, vice president and chair of the main sanctuary's building committee, to ask Dr. Kamenir to oversee the project and serve as liaison between temple, architect, and construction company.

Groundbreaking took place the same week as the Six Day War in Israel. The joy and excitement of Sinai's expansion, which should have been the highlight of the moment, was eclipsed by tremendous panic and fear. Throughout Los Angeles (and all around the world), urgent appeals went out to raise money for the war effort. Rabbi Silverman, who person-

Ark interior

ally fought for Israel's independence, worked hard to assure her survival by supporting a massive, urgent fundraising effort on behalf of Israel Bonds.

Separately, Phase II of the Sinai building fund campaign netted $82,000 in Israel Bonds signed over to the temple, but the board felt it was morally wrong to cash them in, given the current crisis. Instead, 36 directors—including Dr. Mitchell Locks, Dr. Marty Mendelsohn, and Mr. Don Shulman—signed personal notes to cover the equivalent amount, thus freeing up those funds for construction to start on time.

Given his thorough understanding of building, plus his innate business acumen, Dr. Kamenir had the brilliant idea to supervise construction of a *four*-story structure instead of the three-story building officially planned. (The temple hoped to add another floor sometime later when the budget would allow.) He accomplished this by using a different kind of steel and stronger beams than had been planned originally, which could then support and sustain a fourth floor. Dr. Kamenir discussed this *only* with Mr. Frank and told him to proceed accordingly and in strictest confidence.

Next, he quietly went to Alex Kraus, saying he could "give him" the whole floor, if he wanted to underwrite it. The Kraus family truly loved Sinai, and Dr. Kamenir put his faith in that devotion. Within a week, Mr. Kraus agreed. Dr. Kamenir went to the board, suggested his plan, and indicated that a member would pledge the money if the board approved the concept. What he knew, of course, was that the fourth floor was already a "done deal" anyway!

"Sinai East"

Construction at the top of Wilshire Boulevard continued uneventfully over the next year. "Sinai East," as 4th and New Hampshire came to be called during the 1960s, continued to provide some social and religious services for those members who stayed with the congregation in that neighborhood. In November 1967, however, it fell victim to arson.

Damages were estimated at more than $10,000 from three small fires in the upstairs classrooms and a major blaze in the main social hall. Fortunately, no one was injured, and the "old" temple was repaired. In fact, from the time the temple moved to Westwood and until the old building was eventually sold, Sinai Temple spent considerable sums of money on structural repairs to maintain the building's safety.

Lives Extinguished in the Late 1960s

Almost nothing else went according to plan for the rest of the country. In April 1968, Dr. Martin Luther King, Jr. was assassinated on a Memphis motel balcony, marking a tragic and violent end to a nonviolent Nobel Peace Prize winner. Two months later in Los Angeles, Senator Robert F. Kennedy—scion of the powerful Kennedy clan—having just won the California presidential primary, was shot to death in the pantry of the Ambassador Hotel.

By the end of the summer, mayhem ruled in Chicago at the Democratic National Convention. Long-haired hippies clashed with shield-wielding police, and the most serious casualty was the traumatic death of any predictable status quo. U.S. nightly news featured urban riots and fires, college campus demonstrations, and soldiers in body bags. A darkness descended with no end in sight.

And then in the autumn, Rabbi Kohn died. Nearly 90 years old, it was not unexpected, but devastating and sad nonetheless. For many congregants, it was like losing a father. He had "always" been there, thoughtfully and steadily contributing to the temple in countless, meaningful ways. For 37 years, Rabbi Kohn played a vital role not just at Sinai Temple, but also across all of Jewish Los Angeles—whether through his founding role at the UJ, his leadership of the Rabbinical Assembly, or through a variety of public and private contributions to the lives of more people than ever could be tallied.

Rabbi Kohn served Sinai Temple humbly, modestly, and well. He dedicated his life to assuring that Sinai Temple represented the pinnacle of Conservative Judaism, and he himself was a shining example of the highest personal character Sinai Temple sought to develop from childhood on.

Rabbi Hillel Silverman

Chapter Ten

Casualties of War

Rabbi Kohn's death marked the end of an era for Sinai, literally and figuratively. It ended 37 years of a father figure sheltering and shepherding the congregation. His death also signaled a time of tremendous change for the country.

Vietnam continued to divide the nation. The year 1968 marked the beginning of a new radicalism in America and, as evidence, the Democratic National Convention was one of the most turbulent political gatherings of the century. In 1969, Woodstock, the music festival that defined a generation, gave birth to free love and liberal attitudes. In the words of Timothy Leary, young people started to "turn on, tune in, and drop out."

The following year, the Governor of Ohio dispatched the National Guard to Kent State

SINAI TEMPLE WELCOMES VIETNAMESE FAMILY OF SEVEN

Beverly Kokin, head of the temple's Social Concerns Committee, and **Belle Landa** welcomed **Phan Lu**, his wife and five children upon their arrival from a refugee camp in Hong Kong. Since the family did not speak English, **Kiet Koang**, an assistant bookkeeper at Sinai, has served as an interpreter. The congregation provided a private tutor and raised enough money to help maintain the **Lu** family for six months.

University, where anti–Vietnam War protests led to a confrontation between the Guard and students, killing four innocent bystanders. This single event polarized the nation into law-and-order supporters vs. anti-Establishment activists, and marked the beginning of real backlash against President Richard Nixon and his policy in Vietnam.

Sinai and Soviet Jewry

With a window into the Soviet Union, the world could see for the first time the desperate status of Soviet Jews. Many of the most educated people—including doctors, scientists, researchers—were Jewish, although they didn't observe their Judaism openly. For years, they tried to leave their country for Israel or any other place where they could live in freedom and practice their faith.

Unfortunately, the Soviet government refused to grant permission to leave since it would cause a tremendous "brain drain." Once "refuseniks" applied to leave, they were usually fired from their jobs and deprived of any opportunity to find another. With no source of income, and shunned by the government, they literally depended on the kindness of friends and strangers for their sustenance.

Sinai Temple, known for its robust commitment to social activism, organized to help Soviet Jews. Rabbi Silverman frequently spoke about the need to support our brethren in the gulag, and congregants made numerous trips there. Commonly, visitors took all sorts of goods that either were unavailable, banned, or unaffordable, and they gave them to members of the Jewish community to either use or sell on the black market to help supplement their income.

Soviet authorities monitored everything coming in and leaving the country, from books and blue jeans to photos and pharmaceuticals. Jews were forbidden to receive prayer books, and, like everyone else, they also lacked adequate medicine. Muriel Moster and her husband, Jules, organized several trips, and Mrs. Moster tells a funny story about one of them. While going only for a two-week journey, she took stockpiles of birth control pills in her suitcase. In the early 1970s, birth control pills were still relatively new in the United States and *very* scarce in the U.S.S.R. When the authorities saw so many of the tiny pills and asked what they were, Mrs. Moster looked at the agents with a poker-straight face and said, "They're my vitamins."

President Nixon was extremely helpful negotiating on behalf of the refuseniks for their release, and for this, Jews were grateful.

Silverman and Gold

Rabbi Silverman contributed to the temple in perhaps the most fundamental way: through his highly persuasive fundraising efforts, he kept money flowing in, which allowed programming to develop and flourish. Rabbi Silverman possessed the most important quality for someone soliciting funds: he absolutely believed in his cause. When he worked on behalf of Sinai Temple, he put his heart and soul into it. He was so charming and so convincing that he never walked away empty-handed.

Rabbi Zvi Dershowitz

Rabbi Silverman contributed to Sinai Temple's success in another extremely important way: he hired Rabbi Zvi Dershowitz. Rabbi Dershowitz still serves today as Rabbi Emeritus and can proudly say that he has been with Sinai Temple for over one-third of its history. Rabbis Silverman and Dershowitz complemented each other with their different strengths and skills coming together for the benefit of the congregation.

Both were staunch Zionists and tremendous advocates of Israel. While they never overtly defined their roles, Rabbi Silverman represented Sinai externally to the community and Rabbi Dershowitz focused internally, anchoring day-to-day activities within its halls. During their partnership, adult education soared; social commitment within and outside the temple increased; youth activities and involvement grew; and the temple experienced an extended period of vibrancy.

Hugo Dershowitz was born on May 4, 1928, in the industrial city of Brno, Czechoslovakia. His given Czech name at

The ever popular auction bazaar.

birth was Hugo, or Hirsch in Yiddish, which translates as the animal "deer," or Zvi, in Hebrew. His businessman father, Aaron, and mother, Aurelia (Ruth), were modern Orthodox, active Zionists, very cosmopolitan and comfortable whether at the opera or in *shul*. Prior to the outbreak of World War II, the Dershowitz family was part of a secret railroad operation that hid people escaping from the Nazis and then sent them off to safety elsewhere.

When Zvi was 10 years old, Germany invaded Czechoslovakia. His grandfather, Sholem, called all his sons together and said, "This one (Hitler) is different. You have to leave." Fearing for their safety, the family fled by train. Eventually, the Dershowitzs moved to Brooklyn, New York, on February 2, 1939 ... just 33 days before Hitler marched into Brno. Other family relations had come to America earlier; some shortened their last name to Dash. One relative was Sam Dash, who served as chief counsel for the House Judiciary Committee during the Watergate hearings; famed attorney Allen Dershowitz is a cousin.

Rabbi Dershowitz was ordained in 1953 from Mesiftah Torah Voda'ath, an Orthodox institution in Brooklyn. Like so many rabbis before him at Sinai, he is multilingual and can speak Hebrew, English, German, Czech, and Yiddish; he also reads a little Russian. This served him well in future travels to the Soviet Union.

Rabbi Dershowitz met his wife, Tova, while he was recruiting summer staff for Camp Solel in Ithica, New York. She was from Scranton, Pennsylvania, and was active in the Junior Congregation of Rabbi Max Arzt. An excellent tutor, she was offered a scholarship to the JTS Teachers' Institute; the couple married and settled briefly in Morristown, New Jersey, when the rabbi received a call from congregation Beth El in Kansas City, Missouri asking him to be youth director at Herzl Camp. Next, he went to Temple of Aaron in St. Paul, Minnesota, where he stayed several years until Brandeis (later Brandeis-Bardin Institute) in Simi Valley, California, recruited him, followed by Camp Ramah in Ojai, California. Rabbi Dershowitz made an excellent name for himself by creating extraordinary learning opportunities in outstanding settings for youths and adults. Wherever they went, Mrs. Dershowitz also taught and earned her own legion of fans.

While at Camp Ramah in Ojai, the rabbi met Dr. Kamenir, one of Sinai's stalwarts, who was chairman for building the new camp. Through their work together, the rabbi became familiar with the temple in Los Angeles and contacted its Men's Club to offer them the camp for a weekend retreat.

Rabbi Silverman attended the retreat because he had a soft spot in his heart for Ramah. Interestingly enough, both rabbis previously worked at Ramah camps, but at different ones, at separate times. When they finally met, they had a tremendous amount in common. The second night of the retreat, Rabbi Silverman had such a great feeling about Rabbi Dershowitz that he asked him to come work at Sinai: it took two years until the timing and circumstances aligned.

Adult Education Flourishes at Sinai

In the interim, Rabbi Silverman asked Rabbi Dershowitz to help with adult education on a part-time basis. For ten

The Shomrei Tarbut Dance Group under the direction of Bobbie Smotrich, sponsored by Sinai's Adult Education Committee, has performed throughout greater Los Angeles.
Left to right: Front row: Judy Fischer, Judy Flax, Golda Mendelsohn, Barbara Camras. Second row: Frankie Edelman, Rachel Laemmle, Pat Barrett, Bobbie Smotrich, Dani Dassa, Gloria Levand, Adele Stogel, Geri Bieber, Betty Kabaker

years, from 1962 to 1972, Rabbi Merritt had brilliantly shaped and directed the program and curriculum. His innovative classes and events created a dynamic culture of learning that drew adults to Sinai and encouraged lifelong education. The synagogue needed someone when Rabbi Merritt left.

Rabbi Dershowitz did just that, contributing in lasting ways over the course of many more years toward the temple's well-deserved reputation of outstanding adult education.

To appreciate the popularity of adult education and its impact on daily life at temple, it's important to understand that at one point, over 600 people were enrolled in classes *out of a congregation of 800 member families!* While each person who registered for a class technically counted as one student, the number of people participating in the program was, nevertheless, enormous relative to the number of synagogue members at the time. Many of the programs, such as the adult bat mitzvah program and "Young Adults" (which is now ATID), Rabbi Dershowitz created years ago still exist today. He also built up a group called "Dignitaires," which is today's "Chai Society."

Rabbi Dershowitz was a good fundraiser in his own right, raising large sums to underwrite lecture series and guest speakers too. And perhaps, most impressively, for a few years, three temples collaborated to offer adult education classes with one combined community brochure. They had strength in numbers and maximized their clout by pooling funds ... especially to bring in high-caliber speakers. The halls of Sinai Temple welcomed and teemed with members of the Jewish community from all over Los Angeles, regardless of temple affiliation or denomination. It was truly a community center.

When Sinai members went to Russia in the mid-1970s, Rabbi Dershowitz sent them (or went himself with his accomplished and much-admired wife) with prayer books and Hebrew books they smuggled in. Many years later on a trip to Israel, the rabbi met a young girl from Minsk at the Dead Sea. She spoke beautiful Hebrew. When he told her he came from Los Angeles, California, she said that fifteen years earlier, Sinai members came to her town with Hebrew books and that is how she learned! Members also managed to secure the release of Dr. Alexander Luntz, an important refusenik who eventually guest lectured to a packed house at Sinai.

ADULT BAT MITZVAH AT SINAI TEMPLE

Featured in the picture, are the members of Sinai Temple's seventh adult B'not Mitzvah class, under the able and dedicated guidance of Cantor Emeritus **Carl Urstein.** This attractive group of young mothers and grandmothers, reached a memorable milestone in their lives in completing one full year of intensive study of Cantillation, Prayer Chants, Zmirot and the Havdallah service.

Upon the completion of their studies, the students participate in a culmination service, on the Sabbath afternoon, for Mincha, in the charming surroundings of Kohn Chapel, our Beth Hamidrash, aglow with the smiling faces of husbands, proud children and grandchildren, friends and guests. At the close of the service, all worshippers are invited to the Seudah Shilishit. The hall is alive with warm fellowship, good fod and lively Zmirot. The chanting of the Bircot Hamazon in unison and the setting of the sun, signals a return to the Kohn Chapel for the Ma-a-riv Service.

New vistas open up for all our B'not Mitzvah. They have taken on added synagogue commitments. They are now called upon to read the Torah on their personal simchas of the year, birthdays, anniversaries, Yarzeits etc.

On the High Holidays, they have become the readers in the overflow service. Each year forges added links to our Bat Mitzvah group. An alumni has been formed, for the purpose of furthering our traditional studies and holding fast to all they have learned.

Sophie Urstein

The 1970s Sound

Cantor Carl Urstein retired in 1972, although he still graced the temple with his presence for many more years and regularly sat on the *bimah*. When he retired, he attempted to secure a small pension for himself since nothing ever had been done to provide such. He and the temple Board eventually negotiated a financial arrangement that would allow the Cantor and his wife some financial independence in their old age.

Up to that point, Sinai Temple had not made advance financial preparations to provide for clergy and their families in old age. This was the case with Cantor Silverman in the 1940s, with Rabbi Kohn when he retired, with Rabbi Chodos and, again, with Cantor Urstein. At each transition, the board had to meet under special circumstances to consider what to do. Fortunately, the Board of Directors has since recognized the need to provide for the financial security of its clergy and employees in their retirement, and it has implemented necessary changes to bring the temple up to competitive standards with similar institutions.

Cantor Joseph Gole

After Cantor Urstein retired, Cantor Joseph Gole came aboard in 1972, bringing with him good sound, good looks, and youthful energy. He was born in 1947, the same year Cantor Urstein joined Congregation Sinai. The son of a Polish survivor, Cantor Gole grew up in a Conservative home that stressed Jewish cultural identity over strict religious observance, although his parents did send him to Hebrew school. He had a beautiful voice even as a child and, from the age of six, his cantor asked him to sing solos in synagogue. Young Joe also played accordion from the age of five, and to this day, he loves Klezmer music.

Joseph Gole, Sinai cantor from 1972–1982, returned to Sinai in 2000.

He followed a secular music career and struggled with the notion of being a full-time cantor, but he accepted the Sinai job at the age of 25. For the first time in about 30 years, two relatively young men led Sinai Temple.

During Cantor Gole's first two years, Sinai held two extraordinary concerts given by two opera legends. One featured Richard Tucker, an internationally acclaimed tenor who also was a renowned *chazzan*; the other soloist was Robert Merrill, who was a leading baritone at the Metropolitan Opera, who passed away in 2004.

Aryell Cohen

Two years after Cantor Gole arrived, another fresh face appeared at the temple: Mr. Aryell Cohen joined Sinai as choir director and organist. He still coaxes beautiful sounds from the four-member choir and the keyboards every Shabbat, on High Holidays, and on other special occasions. Cantor Urstein personally trained Mr. Cohen (who everyone but his students refers to by first name), and in memory of his beloved teacher, Aryell keeps a photo of him on his office wall, sharing the impressive legacy of "Sinai Sound" with each bar and bat mitzvah he helps prepare. Having been with Sinai for 35 years now himself, Mr. Cohen is also an integral part of the temple's rich musical history.

Just as an excellent cantor interprets the prayers to deliver more than just Hebrew words put to music, so, too, does Mr. Cohen know the meaning of the service and its melodies. He has a distinct, lyrical touch when he plays the organ, adding tremendous depth of feeling to the notes, embellishing phrases and bringing warmth and majesty to what we hear.

Akiba Academy: The Early Years

Not long after the new building opened, board president Dr. Kamenir noticed that it stood essentially empty during the day. It only saw active use during evenings, on Sundays, and for Hebrew and religious school. This seemed like a waste of resources to him. He walked Rabbi Silverman through the empty hallways one day and asked if he knew of a struggling day school that might benefit from a wonderful "home." Rabbi Silverman came back to Dr. Kamenir a week later with the name of Akiba Academy, just starting and still without a permanent location.

Shortly thereafter, Sinai Temple offered its facilities to Akiba Academy and thus began a relationship that would deepen over the years. The affiliation with Akiba Academy brought great prestige to Sinai Temple because it was the one area of children's education the temple did not offer.

Hannah and David Lippert.

The Temple's Guiding Lights

Sinai Temple was guided into the 1970s under the steady and strong influence of its then-president, Dr. Kamenir. Dr. Gerald Freeman took the reins from him and kept the temple on an upward course for the next two years. Judge David I. Lippert, who joined Sinai as a teenager, became president in 1973, to the delight of everyone. Married to Major Hannah Lippert, Judge Lippert was equally respected as his wife and truly loved by all. His exceptional record keeping and attention to detail provided essential information for this book.

Herman Friedberg and then William Friedland each served as president after that. No one could know it at the time, but the end of the 1970s would be the end of what might be considered the Ashkenazi Era at Sinai. Everything that "defined" the temple in terms of its customs, traditions, and idiosyncrasies was about to change due to a sudden and unexpected event halfway around the world.

From School Days to Shul *Daze*

In the late 1970s, politics in Iran shifted. Conditions for Jews began to deteriorate, and many Persian Jews began to flee—primarily for Israel, New York, and Los Angeles—knowing they were no longer safe in their homeland. Thriving exile communities already existed in those places, so it made sense to relocate there.

Sinai Temple had several Persian members of longstanding, and it appealed to many Iranian arrivals. An influx of new people began attending services, or, rather, showing up on Friday nights and Shabbat mornings. They arrived late and stayed late, often skipping services completely to meet friends in the lobby and get news from home. After all, they were refugees from a nation in revolution. No one knew from week to week who had escaped, whether they had gotten out unharmed, or where they had gone.

The increased Persian presence altered the rhythm of life at the temple because in Persian culture things typically start late and run into the early hours of the morning. In an attempt to get the newcomers to leave early, the lights were turned off soon after Friday night services ended.

Sinai regulars complained: noise levels had risen; the hallways swelled with people who didn't speak English. What many people forgot was that Sinai Temple began as an amalgam of people from different nations speaking different languages. They just happened to come from Europe instead of the Middle East. When Farsi filled the air, instead of hearing the voice of fellow Jews once again displaced from their land and everything familiar, countless people at Sinai unfortunately responded with coldness and insensitivity, and, in some instances, outright hostility. Shabbat became a time of tension instead of peace. Problems arose from a distinct clash of cultures and style.

Joining vs. Shnoddering

In the United States, Jews "join" a temple by becoming a member and then paying annual dues. In Iran, the system was different. Synagogues were "free" and the custom was to pay when given an *aliyah*. Whether a baby was born, a wedding took place, or a funeral occurred, Persian custom called for family and friends to donate for the occasion—very much like the past practice of *shnoddering*. But few people at Sinai could remember back that far.

As more and more immigrants arrived, several "old timers" (and even many not-so-old-timers) took it hard. Sinai-ites felt as if their home was being invaded by outsiders, and they were being forced to adapt. For the Persians arriving from Iran, it was difficult to understand what they possibly could have done to engender such unfriendliness. They were delighted to come to Sinai and grateful for the freedom that allowed it.

Synagogues have always been meeting places for, among other things, the exchange of information ... a safe house of refuge for any Jew. All Jews know from our collective cultural history, if not personally, what it is to be unwelcome or even persecuted. As the two distinct communities have grown to understand, love, and even marry each other over the past 25 years, we have come to know—deeply and happily—that cultural and linguistic differences are but poor camouflage of our spiritual sameness and holiness in the sight of God.

Shalom

During this time, Rabbi Silverman did his best to integrate the influx of Persian Jews. Wherever possible, he extended a helping hand to those in need when they arrived. While Sinai today has a reputation for having extremely wealthy Persian members, many had lost everything—material wealth being the least of their sacrifices. Some had witnessed, or experienced, unspeakable horrors and brutality and faced tremendous challenges trying to reconcile their fate and keep faith in a god who would let such atrocities occur. In fact, many outcast Persians shared a great deal—whether or not people recognized it—with other survivors in the congregation. They just couldn't speak the same language to discover it.

Doris Siegel

Iranian Jews tried to make a fresh start in Los Angeles, and Sinai Temple, presciently designed like a tent in the desert, became their oasis. But like most oasis sanctuaries, that image was really a mirage. In truth, a sandstorm was brewing that few saw coming and even fewer could believe after being blindsided.

Rabbi Silverman had personal issues, which resulted in his moving out of his home, and resigning as Rabbi of Sinai. He moved to another congregation, remarried, and eventually pursued a fresh start in Connecticut, where he still serves on a part-time emeritus basis.

His departure shocked and saddened the congregation that admired and looked up to him for sixteen years. Then–president Doris Siegel called Rabbi Dershowitz, who was in Israel at the time. He took the first flight back to Los Angeles and began to resuscitate the stricken synagogue.

Mrs. Siegel generously found ways to donate her time and talents to Sinai Temple for the rest of her life ... even during her last two years while suffering severe health problems. When Mrs. Siegel passed away in 2005, Sinai Temple paid her its highest tribute for her tireless contributions over 50 years: her funeral took place in the Ruth and Allen Ziegler Sanctuary, a very rare honor, indeed.

Kehillat Hodve Hadar—Sinai's Sister Synagogue in Israel

Chapter Eleven

Hot Seats and Musical Chairs

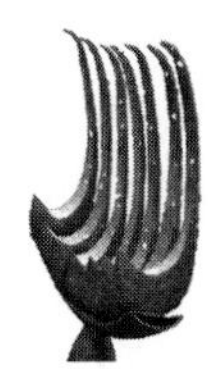

Rabbi Dershowitz stepped up to the *bimah* and took over admirably. Many practical issues had to be addressed, not the least of which was the reassignment of roles and responsibilities. As had happened several times before, going from two rabbis to one left the remaining cleric with more work than he could possibly handle alone.

A large part of his duties included supervising and conducting adult education classes. Rabbi Dershowitz realized quickly he would have to reduce, if not suspend, his involvement with these classes to accommodate all the other tasks that now fell to him.

For eighteen months and with no assistant himself, Rabbi Dershowitz did the very best he could as the interim rabbi, helping the synagogue heal and move forward. Unbeknownst to anyone then, this is a role he would repeat more than once in the future. Because he was quite content to remain Sinai's associate rabbi, the temple began looking for a new senior clergyman. No matter who took the post, it would be a challenge since congregants would naturally compare him with Rabbi Silverman. No one could foresee just how tough it would be.

Rabbi Solomon Rothstein

Rabbi Solomon Rothstein (pronounced Roth-steen) joined Sinai Temple in 1981. Born in the Bronx, New York, and a 1956 graduate of JTS, he began his career at The Jewish Community Center of Fort Lee, in New Jersey, while still a student at the seminary. Starting with just 25 families, the Fort Lee congregation grew to over 1,000 families during the 29 years of Rabbi Rothstein's leadership. Bicoastal comedian Buddy Hackett was a member of his congregation and encouraged Rabbi Rothstein to apply for the rabbinic opening in L.A., but the rabbi wasn't anxious to leave a lifetime contract that afforded him tremendous autonomy.

Allen Ziegler went to New Jersey to recruit the rabbi. Rabbi Rothstein was intrigued by the possibility of helping a congregation in transition move forward after its previous turmoil. He came to Los Angeles, met several of the board members and, while he was candidly advised that it would take years for the congregation to "quiet down" in the wake of Rabbi Silverman's sudden departure, he was equally assured that the congregation was ready to move forward.

With the experience and respect that nearly 30 years as a senior rabbi had brought him, Rabbi Rothstein felt confident that he could help Sinai heal, grow, and prosper. In 1981, he came to Los Angeles with his wife, Beverly, and the youngest of their four children.

His arrival couldn't have been more propitious. People were warm and hospitable to the new rabbi and his wife, and it appeared Sinai was, indeed, ready to move forward.

Off to a Good Start ...

Rabbi Rothstein started off well, working hard to restore a sense of cohesion amongst the congregants and refocus everyone on goals for the future, rather than events of the recent past. He spoke at length, 25 years ago, of Sinai becoming a synagogue-

center, offering not just worship, but also a well-rounded Jewish
communal environment in which to learn and live. Los Angeles had a Jewish population of half a million at the time, and Rabbi Rothstein wanted Sinai to have something for everybody—preschoolers to college students, young marrieds and retirees.

He made an excellent first impression. His vision for the temple's future was ambitious, but perfectly in line with board objectives. Rabbi Rothstein was also a clinical psychologist: this gave him additional skills with which to effectively communicate. One of the ways he and Mrs. Rothstein tried to build bridges was by opening their home to congregants for Shabbat dinner, giving as many people as possible the opportunity to express their opinions about the direction in which the temple should go.

Membership at Sinai had plummeted after Rabbi Silverman left, so the new rabbi focused on increasing membership, especially among singles and young families. But the high cost of membership seemed prohibitive to people just starting out. Westwood was still a developing neighborhood: the rabbi suggested an introductory $99 membership and special dues structure for young people since so many lived nearby. Some board members balked at the idea, but Rabbi Rothstein persisted, and it paid off—membership grew to 1,475 within three years of his arrival.

Both Friday night and Saturday morning services were heavily attended, and Rabbi Rothstein remembers speaking from the pulpit as one of his job's highlights. As part of his commitment to young people, he instituted special fourth-floor High Holiday services just for them. These services were more informal, and the crowds they attracted proved the rabbi's decision was correct. He also oversaw the development of Saturday night functions, which were quite successful with young families, and he brought back the ever-popular adult education programs, which had a brief hiatus when Rabbi Dershowitz temporarily redirected his energies after Rabbi Silverman left.

But Then ... SOS

In theory, everything should have worked out. But in retrospect, anybody coming in after the upheaval of Rabbi Silverman's sudden departure probably would have found it difficult.

At Sinai, conflict arose between the rabbi and the cantor, whose contract was up for renewal shortly after the new rabbi arrived. As with any disagreement, two explanations or more always exist as to "what happened." Some people insist Rabbi Rothstein wanted to oust Cantor Gole and hire someone of his own choosing. Rabbi Rothstein asserts he respected Cantor Gole and admired his beautiful voice, and had only positive feelings for him. The situation was made more difficult because Cantor Gole had obtained his license as a Realtor® and was beginning to be successful at it. Many in the congregation and/or on the board felt he shouldn't do both jobs.

Tensions arose between the two men causing an adversarial relationship that began to affect their performance. The board didn't want to antagonize its recently installed rabbi, so it solved the problem the easiest way possible: by letting time run its course. When the time came to begin negotiations to renew Cantor Gole's contract, it simply didn't. The cantor plainly understood the "no confidence" message and left, which infuriated those members who supported him. For the first time in its history, the congregation began to split apart.

His departure gave birth to a movement called Save Our Sinai, or "SOS," which nearly sank Sinai. Comprised of members who believed Sinai was wrong to "acquiesce" to the new rabbi, SOS was founded with the intention of either reinstating Cantor Gole or, as a last resort, creating a splinter, breakaway congregation.

SOS held meetings off-site at the Beverly Hills High School auditorium, at congregants' homes, and at other nearby venues where members passionately discussed what to do. The situation became so volatile (SOS *vs.* the Establishment) that lifelong friends with differing opinions ostracized each other; neighbors stopped speaking with neighbors; and some long-standing davening buddies in the main sanctuary asked for seat reassignment.

SOS recruited nearly half the congregation, and its threat affected everyone. Tremendous negative energy enveloped the entire temple and brought with it all the attendant negative publicity one would expect. Open wounds needed immediate attention to avoid festering.

The first, and most logical, place to start was at the board level. Serious bridge building was required. SOS leadership insisted the makeup of the board should more fairly represent them: the group did not have adequate representation on the board, at least not in a number proportionate to the number of people within the congregation who endorsed its viewpoint and shared its concerns.

The solution (which seems to have resulted from an outright threat of mutiny) was to reconstruct the board with half the members coming from SOS, as well as a future president who also came from the

SOS ranks. The state of affairs had become so acrimonious, in fact, that the next several presidents of the board were predetermined—not by individual identity, but by whether or not they represented pro-SOS or Establishment constituents.

A New Voice at Sinai: Cantor Finkelstein

With the departure of Cantor Gole, Rabbi Rothstein really needed to find another *chazzan*. The temple turned to another young man, this one a bona fide star in the grand tradition of Sinai musicianship: Meir Finkelstein (pronounced May-eer Finkelsteen). Born in Israel in 1951, he moved with his family to London as a youngster and followed in his father's footsteps, also becoming a cantor. But his father, Zvi, hadn't started at the age of 14, which was when his son took his first job as cantor of the synagogue in Glasgow, Scotland, making him the youngest cantor ever in all of Europe.

The prestigious Golders Green Synagogue in London next hired him. Later, with a scholarship to, and professional training at, the Royal Academy of Music in London, Meir graduated with honors, skilled in composition as well as singing. Prior to joining Sinai, Cantor Finkelstein performed in concert extensively throughout the United States, covering both classical and liturgical repertoires. He approached every song as an opportunity for musical excellence and brought extraordinary sound to Sinai, with high technical

Cantor Finkelstein

performance. He also composed prolifically and, even today, Sinai services incorporate many of his melodies. Sinai was enchanted with Cantor Finkelstein and asked him to perform whenever possible.

Uplifting music was the perfect accompaniment for the 1980s, which brought long awaited growth and prosperity to the United States, the likes of which hadn't been experienced almost since the Roaring Twenties. Money couldn't be printed fast enough before it was spent on real estate, fashion, the stock market, or the latest trendy restaurants. Young professionals made higher annual salaries than their parents earned in a lifetime.

Ronald Reagan swept into office, bringing with him a homespun "can do" spirit that invigorated America. Known as the "Great Communicator," he talked to the country in his polished actor's voice and made people believe anything was possible.

Amazing things were possible. The 1980s produced medical miracles such as the eradication of smallpox; "ET" phoned home; Apple introduced the Macintosh computer; Madonna became a pop diva; and Elie Wiesel won the Nobel Peace Prize.

President Reagan's reassurance was important because many awful things happened during this period. In 1981 alone, Anwar Sadat was assassinated; Central America struggled with multinational civil unrest; Israel bombed a nuclear plant in Iraq (for which the UN Security Council condemned it); and Reagan was shot in an assassination attempt from which he recovered, but that permanently crippled his press secretary, James Brady.

In addition, many Sinai congregants monitored the volatile situation in Iran with great interest and concern. Iraq invaded Iran in 1980. The next year, Muslim leftists killed the president, prime minister, and 29 others with a bomb; in 1986, the U.S. government admitted to an illegal arms-for-hostages deal involving Iran and Nicaragua; and in 1988, Iran and Iraq finally agreed to a peace plan.

With so much upheaval all around, it is no wonder that people were agitated and stressed. Such conditions often led to criticism. Something had to give, and in this case, the something was some*one*. Rabbi Rothstein had come to Los Angeles with the best of intentions, under the impression he would be the head of a powerful congregation, and he had started off well. But as time went on, and especially in the aftermath of SOS, he often found his efforts thwarted. Whether or not it fairly can be attributed to him, the congregation nearly unraveled under his stewardship. The board finally said, "Enough."

With only six months remaining of the rabbi's three-year contract, the temple informed the rabbi that his contract would not be renewed. He and Sinai Temple parted ways. He went to another congregation in the Valley and, eventually, retired to Florida where he lives today. Rabbi Rothstein's ex-wife still attends Sinai Temple on the High Holidays and has many dear friends, including the Elephant Ladies—Jean Powell, Millie Cohen, Barbara Blaine, Ruth Pilot, Renee Diamond, and Pearl Goldberg—who all wear the same ivory elephant friendship necklace and lunch together on each other's birthday.

Moshe Tutnauer: The Rescue Rabbi

After Rabbi Rothstein left in 1984, the temple brought in Rabbi Moshe Tutnauer. Well-liked throughout the Conservative movement, he is frequently hired by synagogues in transition as an interim rabbi while the congregation searches for a permanent replacement. Typically, he stays only eight months, and lives in Israel the rest of the year. Rabbi Tutnauer has an easy-going manner and dresses like a typical Israeli—in short sleeve shirts, without a tie—very casual compared to the formality for which Sinai is known.

Sinai liked Rabbi Tutnauer and his wife, Margie, so much that the board asked him to stay on permanently. When he declined the offer, reminding people of his life in Israel, Sinai actually offered him an 8-month-per-year contract, saying it would find alternative coverage over the summer months, but he again declined such an arrangement. Nevertheless, he ended up staying for almost two years and is a beloved friend of many congregants even today.

Sinai Temple and Akiba Academy

On May 20, 1986, Sinai Temple officially "married" Akiba Academy, after having "lived together" for eighteen years. Dr. Ezra Novak and Milo Mandel negotiated the *shiddach* that finally gave Sinai Temple the school it needed to complete its portfolio as a full-service, leading Conservative synagogue. The school's new name became Sinai Akiba Academy (SAA), a Solomon Schechter day school. In recognition of the excellence of SAA, the preschool, Douglas Family Early Education Center (DFECC), was placed under the aegis of SAA.

Sinai Temple gained tremendous prestige by, at last, having its own day school. In the 20 years since the merger, SAA has grown tremendously and has served as a significant, if not the primary, driver of membership to the synagogue. Only members in good standing may send

their children there, and many people initially join the *shul* for this reason. One of Sinai's greatest challenges lies in creating a stimulating communal adult environment for families to stay after their children leave school. In recent years, many parents of former students have risen through the ranks and become board members and leaders of Sinai Temple.

SAA describes itself as "a school for the mind, the heart, the soul." With a well-rounded curriculum that includes everything from art classes to science, drama, mathematics, and Torah study, it graduates pupils with a love of learning, high academic achievement, and an excellent foundation in Judaic studies. Because SAA currently only educates through eighth grade, students must finish their secondary education elsewhere, but they regularly gain acceptance at Ivy League, Pac-10, and other excellent universities. SAA tries to maintain contact with alumni through an increasingly active alumni association. Several alumni have returned as parents or staff.

Rabbi Laurence Scheindlin has skillfully guided the school as headmaster since 1977. In addition to his many outstanding quantifiable accomplishments, he has also created an important intangible: a positive learning environment for the children, and a stable and pleasant working atmosphere for the stellar roster of teachers who provide the daily backbone. Rivka Shaked, Vivian Levy, and Edie Schwartz each have taught at the school for over 30 years (Mrs. Shaked for 40!), instructing not only some of today's students, but in some cases, their parents, as well.

The Libraries of Sinai

> *"Make your books your companions; let your cases and shelves be your pleasure-gardens and orchards. Bask in their paradise, gather their fruit, pluck their roses, take their spices. If your soul be satiate and weary, change from garden to garden, from furrow to furrow, from prospect to prospect. Then will your desire be renewed, and your soul be filled with delight."*
>
> *Ibn Tibbon Tzavaah, 1190*

Jews are often called the People of the Book. We venerate the Torah, not so much as an object, but for the knowledge it contains and the wisdom it imparts. Our love for the Torah extends to books in general, the pleasure they give, and the enrichment that derives from written expression. Children who learn to love books love to learn. Nothing plays a larger role in education than the ability to read.

The First Library

A library is a reflection of what we think is important, worth knowing, worth teaching, and worth preserving. The first Sinai library was at 4th and New Hampshire, and dedicated in 1939 in memory of Hannah and Moses Tannenbaum by their children. It was a small room upstairs in the school building, with a large skylight in the center to help illuminate the room with natural light. Compared to libraries of today, it seems miniscule with only about 200 volumes, but in its time, it was used and appreciated. While a library exists to preserve history through the written word, the memory of Tannenbaum Library might itself have been lost to history were it not for the original bronze dedication plate that was recently recovered from an obscure file cabinet in the current temple's garage.

During the interim period between 4th and New Hampshire and Sinai's arrival in Westwood, Sinai schools were "homeless." Religious and Hebrew school classes were conducted all across the city, with some still being held in the old temple, some on LaCienega, some on Robertson, and eventually, at the empty motel next door to the new main sanctuary. All schools and students finally came together post-1969 in the new school and administration building. The "adults' library" was separate from the school library, remaining, essentially, a small collection of reference and textbooks housed at the motel for teachers' use in their lesson planning.

A New Library

Once the temple completed its move to Wilshire and Beverly Glen, it needed a brand-new library, if it was to have one at all.

There was actually discussion about the necessity, which is hard to imagine today in light of the current library's regular use and excellent reputation. One of the discussion points concerned its location.

Several people lobbied for the library to be located on the main floor. Easy access would make it a natural meeting place for adults who came into the temple for business or classes during the week, as well as for students. Visibility would promote circulation, donations, and a vibrant sense of community. The current popularity of bookstore–coffee shop combinations gives credence to that argument, which just may have been ahead of its time.

Ultimately, the library was housed on the third floor, away from general foot traffic, but more readily accessible to students. Rabbi Daniel Merritt deserves credit for getting the board not only to validate

the importance of having an excellent library, but also to allocate the necessary budget to support it with a professional staff. He further rallied the school to maintain the collection and nurture its growth.

William R. Blumenthal, for whom the library is named today, was its major benefactor even before it was a "real" library. Perhaps his donation inspired action to create one. A true bibliophile and author himself, Mr. Blumenthal donated over 1,000 volumes to Sinai from his own extraordinary book collection. His gift included rare incunabula (books created before 1501...), along with rare Judaica volumes and other precious resources.

At one point in time, the synagogue actually owned an original page from the Gutenberg Bible, donated by Sam Steinberg in honor of his friend, Will Blumenthal. Contrary to popular belief, Mr. Blumenthal did not donate it himself, according to Aviva Ellis-Namir, a long-time member of the temple and close friend of Mr. Blumenthal. Curiously, the temple did not secure this priceless treasure well enough to prevent multiple disappearances (and, even more curiously, repeated safe recoveries, sans ransom or any damage). Finally, exhausted from the high maintenance that such a coveted collectable seemed to require, Mr. Steinberg took it back, and sold it. He used the proceeds to purchase and donate a rare Seder plate to the temple.

The Library Committee

As an adjunct to its new modern library, the board established a library committee, charging it to create and oversee the library's budget and all its activities. The library director ran the library and performed all the typical duties of a librarian; the library committee set the tone and vision for what the library would become in terms of programming and events.

Committee members made themselves available to assist the librarian as much as possible. Serving on the library committee conferred a high degree of respect upon a temple member because it implicitly endorsed someone's own education and commitment to learning. Today, the committee is very active in planning programs, such as book signings and movie discussions. Every year since 1980, the library committee has also held a Jewish Book Month event, originally a special Shabbat and open house. Recently, this has become a breakfast that features an author (with a book signing) and honors outstanding temple members and library patrons.

The Library Staff and Programs

Cecelia Lapidus was the first librarian at 4th and New Hampshire, and the value of her groundwork in establishing the library cannot be overstated. When she retired in 1979 after 34 years of service to Sinai (including her years as a Hebrew teacher), the library search committee—then comprised of Mrs. Moster, Rabbi Merritt, Mr. Jules Porter, and Mrs. Ellis-Namir—selected Mrs. Rita Berman Frischer as her successor. Starting in 1980, Mrs. Frischer nurtured the library for 20 years, propelling it from an ambitious, but underutilized assemblage of books and materials into a professionally organized, computerized, catalogued collection, dedicated to outreach, that continues to grow in size and esteem.

In 1986, the library became the first department of the temple to implement personal computers as an integral part of

Sinai's first full-time librarian, Cecelia Lapidus.

Ritual director Nicholas Mermell and Rita Frischer in the library for Jewish Book Month.

its operation. That same year, it received a grant to establish a central cataloguing service (CCS) for sharing Judaica cataloguing with small synagogue libraries around the country. Yale and New York University, among many other educational institutions with outstanding library science programs, acknowledged Sinai's CCS as a breakthrough service for libraries of Judaica.

A recognized leader in her field, Mrs. Frischer employed all the best practices learned through her active participation in the national Association of Jewish Libraries to turn Sinai Temple's Blumenthal Library into a model among lending libraries, both secular and religious. It has received advanced accreditation by the Jewish Book Council and the Association of Jewish Libraries since 1980. In addition, in 1983, United Synagogue added its Solomon Schechter Award to recognize the excellence attained by the library in serving the religious school, congregation, and the community.

In addition to the outstanding work Mrs. Frischer provided to Sinai, she also shared her expertise with others around the world, lecturing at Bar Ilan University in Israel and for WZO in Australia. In 1988, at the request of Sinai member Dr. George Shecter, she quietly volunteered to consult and help design the library for a medical training school for nurses in Malawi, South Africa. Her input "saved the new school much money and resulted in the master planning of a splendid facility which would not have been realized without her assistance," according to Sinai Temple board minutes. With mixed feelings, but tremendous pride, and with the appreciation and gratitude of Sinai and Sinai Akiba Academy, she retired in 2000 to spend more time with her family.

Today, Lisa Silverman runs the Blumenthal Library, which is larger than any other synagogue library in town, and oversees a staff of six. The number of holdings has grown to nearly 32,000—including books, periodicals, audio, video, and other new media. Almost 2,000 registered patrons, including adults and students, use the facility annually. Joel Tuchman, a staff member and Judaica expert, provides definitive answers to anyone in need of specific information from a vast array of esoteric reference sources.

Mrs. Silverman, whose expertise is in Jewish children's literature, works very hard to create exciting library programs for the students and the congregation and bring the most outstanding books, films, and authors to the temple. For the last three years, Sinai Temple has organized and run the West Coast Jewish Children's Literature Conference.

There is a special reading area for young children, who especially love Shari Charalambous, better known as "Miss Purple" for her dependable, daily fashion statement. Miss Purple has a special relationship with the youngsters, who race to sit on the colorful "Story-time Steps" during monthly pajama nights or read-alongs. This area is decorated with an extraordinary hand-painted chair donated by Gilda Lappe, which, along with a beautiful mural on the wall, contributes to a warm and happy atmosphere conducive to reading, research, and reflection.

Sinai Akiba Academy librarian, Shari Charalambous, with her students.

By the late 1980s, Sinai Temple had almost everything going for it ... except a permanent rabbi. To paraphrase Dorothy from *The Wizard of Oz*, sometimes what you're looking for is right in your own back yard. North in San Francisco, a young rabbi caught the attention of Sinai. His name was Allan Schranz.

Rabbi Allan Schranz and Rabbi Zvi Dershowitz with young Torah readers.

Chapter Twelve

A Change of Heart

Rabbi Allan Schranz served Congregation Beth Sholom in San Francisco. Bright, young, and scholarly, he caught the attention of Rabbi David Lieber, by then president of the UJ, who recommended him. Aaron Fenton and Abner Goldstine went to observe Rabbi Schranz in his own surroundings and, then, on a second trip, Dr. Malcolm Cosgrove and Mr. Milo Mandel joined them. Impressed, they reported back to Sinai: they found someone who could lead the congregation and move it forward.

Rabbi Schranz's career began straight out of rabbinic school as an assistant for two years to JTS chancellor Gerson Cohen. He received his first full-time pulpit at Temple Israel in Ridgewood, New Jersey, where he stayed for nine productive years until San Francisco beckoned.

Rabbi Schranz heeded the call and moved west, and in July 1986, he and his wife, Ellen, with their toddler, Molly, moved to Los Angeles to join Sinai. A son, Asher, would be born a few years later.

A Welcome in Westwood

Rabbi Schranz arrived and found a busy congregation. Sisterhood raised great sums of money for Sinai, making, for instance, a gift of $10,000 to start a computer center at the day school. The synagogue's social action committee put on the first AIDS program in June of 1987, covering the Jewish point of view on issues such as sexuality, relationships, health care, comfort, and sorrow. And Milton Hyman, who would become Sinai President from 1993–1995, urged the development of a formal commemoration ceremony for Yom HaShoah.

Rabbi Schranz worked hard to bring peace to Sinai. He was the third senior rabbi to anchor its *bimah* in six years, and members were in serious need of a spiritual leader who could create a stable environment that supported progress. Although he was relatively young, Rabbi Schranz had a serious nature and quiet demeanor. With his scholarly *d'ivrei torah* during Shabbat services and at the start of board meetings, he supplied food for thought that whetted the congregation's appetite. Many of his intellectual sermons included passages of poetry, leading some worshippers to admit that they didn't understand everything he said, but they thought it sounded beautiful.

Because Torah study holds such a place of high honor, many congregants wanted the opportunity to prepare a *d'var torah* for Shabbat services. From 1987 until 1989, on the third Shabbat of each month, one congregant, instead of the rabbi, would research a Torah portion and deliver the *d'var torah*. Completely self-motivated, these were expertly researched, carefully delivered, and greatly appreciated by the membership. Drs. George Shecter and Ezra Novak—original "Back Benchers"—conceived and supervised the program.

The "Back Bench"

The Back Benchers were a group of lively, opinionated, and knowledgeable congregants. People such as Dr. Max Astrachan, Will Blumenthal, Aviva Ellis-Namir, Dr. Victor and Anna Goodhill, Major Hannah and Judge David Lippert, Dr. Mitchell Locks, Dr. Norman Mirman, and Sol Tuch occupied the second to last pew in the main sanctuary's left center section. (Drs. Locks and Mirman and Mr. Tuch still do.) There, they would *kibbitz* among themselves about goings-on at the temple, and they would have their own discussions about the weekly *parasha*.

For a short time, they placed "reserved" signs on their seats, but this led to a near riot from other members who accused them of elitism ... and then promptly mimicked them by reserving their own seats. The notion of reserving was finally abolished altogether by temple management.

As for the populist *d'ivrei torah*, two volumes of material were ultimately collected and bound and are now located in the temple's archives. They provide fascinating and informative reading and testify to the high standards this congregation sets for itself with regard to Judaic intellectual pursuit.

While this particular "program" was phased out after two years, the temple phased in something else that has remained: multiple *minyanim* that give congregants a choice in their religious expression. Rabbi Schranz supervised these various *minyanim* in an effort to reach out and be as inclusive as possible to existing and potential membership.

Something for Everyone

Sinai, if not unique, was certainly exceptional in that it offered—and still does—a variety of styles of concurrent Shabbat worship, all within the Conservative context. Whether members sought a formal service with traditional melodies sung by the cantor and backed by the choir and organ, or a peer-led service with modern tunes strummed on a guitar, or an informal family service replete with the joyful sounds of toddlers and teenagers, they could find it, and worship, at Sinai.

According to Dr. Arnold Gilberg, a long-time Sinai member who served as financial secretary for six years, and was on the board as well as the board of governors, Rabbi Schranz further distinguished himself by being one of the only rabbis in the city to reach out to poor Jews and minister to their spirituality, not making any class distinction among his flock. He also instigated conversation with parents of intermarried couples to help however they needed, and he thoughtfully made sure that community members had a place to go for Seder. Everything was running smoothly, but soon Rabbi Schranz would be facing health issues that would require immediate attention.

One of the special services his predecessor, Rabbi Rothstein, implemented for the High Holidays, and which continued during Rabbi Schranz's day, was a service held on the fourth floor for young adults and families. Originally led by a young

Members of Sinai's student newspaper pose with Don Rickles after an interview. From left to right: Julie Feinstein, Robert Hurwitz, Don Rickles, Elizabeth Joseph, Greg Wagner, and Laird Malamed. Rick Menashe, the advisor, is not pictured.

man still in rabbinic school, this future rabbi mesmerized and inspired everyone who listened to his outstanding sermons. Attendance grew with each subsequent year he preached.

It seemed clear that this young rabbinic student would go places, and, indeed, when he completed school in 1987, he became a Finkelstein Fellow at the UJ for two years and assistant to the president of the UJ and director of its Ostrow Library for six years. Only then did he become assistant to the chancellor of the seminary in New York. For a brief moment, Sinai feared he wouldn't return to help during the High Holidays. But when it offered to rehire him, he accepted. His name: Rabbi David Wolpe.

In the Red, Once Again

Try as it did to provide members with a vibrant temple, excellent services, and responsive programming, Sinai could not avoid the economic wake-up call of 1989. Much of the financial exuberance of the 1980s had been fueled by aggressive foreign investment. When many of those investors suddenly pulled out of the market, numerous businesses crashed and many people declared bankruptcy. "Debt" became a word heard often.

This reversal of fortune was most definitely felt in terms of day-to-day operations. Due to advancing inflation, Sinai found itself, once again, spending money it didn't have. Provisions were made for tem-

Ruth Ziegler surrounded by SAA girl scouts.

porarily operating in the red—all nonessential costs were cut, but the deficit still ran in the hundreds of thousands of dollars and lasted for several years, much to everyone's consternation. In the meantime, different ways were tried to increase revenue. The first and obvious was to increase membership.

Rabbi Rothstein had earlier identified young people as the primary demographic to reach. It presented the greatest challenge. His reduced rate membership for young people was implemented with only limited success. With enormous deficits looming ahead, Dr. Ezra Novak now proposed offering a new "Taste of Sinai," a special one-time only $99 discounted associate membership as a way of attracting young, unaffiliated people. This membership would include a single seat at the fourth-floor High Holiday service, and it would give these members access, although still for a fee, to the many exciting programs held at Sinai.

The board was not thrilled by this prospect because it suspected most people would not renew their "trial" membership at the much higher regular price. On the other hand, the Wolpe services had proved quite popular. It was a calculated risk, but the board was willing to try.

Kraus Youth and Education Center

The Kraus Youth and Education Center (aka Kraus Pavilion)—the fourth floor of the school and administration building—finally opened. Initially conceived as the "extra" floor when Dr. Kamenir oversaw Phase II construction, it took nearly 20 years to raise sufficient funds to outfit the structural shell that had patiently awaited completion.

Unfortunately, Mr. Alex Kraus—one of the founders of California's custom-car culture and world renowned for inventing hanging, fuzzy dice and "Candy Apple Red," the first metallic car paint—had passed away in the interim, but his wife, Lillian, dedicated the Pavilion in his memory at a beautiful ceremony. Kraus Pavilion includes a youth lounge, kitchen facilities, classrooms, and the Rickles Gym, named for comedian Don Rickles and his wife, Barbara, in honor of the benefit performance of stars that Mr. Rickles organized to raise funds for its completion. Technically speaking, Rickles Gym is where David Wolpe conducted the fourth-floor High Holiday services and where they are held today.

A Wealth of Good Causes

Other ways of raising money included increasing dues and holding fundraisers. Unfortunately, as the community grew, overlapping events for different causes or organizations were sometimes scheduled on the same date, which stretched the patience, goodwill, and resources of congregants. Many of them indicated, none-too-subtly, that they were getting "tapped out."

Dorothy Salkin, a hardworking member of the board, created the first comprehensive, year-round programming schedule, along with a budget. She submitted this figure to the board and, for the first time, a true picture emerged of Sinai's enormous commitment to its members and the community at large. Moreover, by finally having this commitment represented as a single budget line and calendar, the board could carefully plan to raise the necessary funds and assure members that Sinai would not double-book important events.

Mrs. Salkin and her husband, Avram, conceived and underwrote an exciting new program called the Rabbi Jacob Kohn Memorial Scholar-In-Residence weekend. It was founded as an annual tribute to a man who illuminated countless lives through his words and deeds for nearly 40 years ... an exceptional scholar and intellectual whose calling to God was expressed through his love of Sinai and its people. This extraordinary program still exists today and has become one of the temple's signature events.

Distinguished intellectuals visit as guest speakers for a full weekend of enlightenment and interaction, speaking on Friday night after dinner, on Shabbat morning briefly during services and again after lunch, and then in dialogue with Rabbi Wolpe on Sunday morning at brunch.

Recently, such luminaries as Leon Wieseltier, Professor Amos Oz, Norman

SAA mensch of the month

Podhoretz, Professor Ruth Wisse, Rabbi Harold Kushner, Sir Martin Gilbert, William Safire, and Dr. Deborah Lipstadt have all made the Kohn Scholar-in-Residence weekends stimulating, memorable, and a sold-out event each year. Past president Abner Goldstine and his wife, Roz, have ensured the viability of this Sinai highlight for the next fifteen years by generously endowing the program until 2020. In recognition, the program has been renamed the Abner and Roslyn Goldstine Scholar-in-Residence Lecture Series.

The Kol Nidre Appeal

The congregation has always had close ties with longstanding Jewish organizations, such as Israel Bonds, Jewish National Fund, and Jewish Federation, as well as the Masorti Movement. Each of them counts on Sinai for support by soliciting funds on its behalf. Board members are explicitly expected to set an example by taking leadership roles in giving.

While it used to be extraordinary and exceptional to ask for money on the holiest night of the year (Rabbi Kohn asked the first time during the Depression, with grave misgivings and only after significant discussion among board members and a vote of approval), it has now become a time-honored tradition that congregants have come to accept and expect. As the sun sets and the stained glass windows framing the *Aron Kodesh* fade from brilliant hues to black, one person stands before the congregation and makes a plea for more. Cash may be the tool of trade (discretely indicated by bending a tab on a card), but commitment is the value and the future is at stake.

This request is anything but cavalier. A contribution is not mandatory, except for board members. Money raised on this one night accounts for nearly 10 percent of the annual budget, and there is never any guarantee that congregants will pledge sufficient funds. The bottom line is that the Kol Nidre Appeal ensures that all of Sinai's programming, plus new innovations, will continue to operate. Everyone is asked to give to the best of his or her own ability.

Membership dues, no matter what amount, never cover everything at any temple. By soliciting funds through the Kol Nidre Appeal, the temple tries to continue running at a high level without increasing dues, potentially causing hardship for some. Responding generously to the Kol Nidre Appeal should be a reflection of true belief in, and appreciation for, the importance of the synagogue and the good work it does.

Catering at Sinai

While the Kol Nidre Appeal is inherently uncertain, one thing Sinai Temple has always banked on is excellent food. From the very beginning of Congregation Sinai, the women have seen to it that no one should ever go hungry. Whether making *oneg Shabbatim*, holiday meals, or anything in between—including the formerly customary Midnight Smorgasbord served after regular monthly board meetings—the ladies of Sinai have truly served.

Today, catering at Sinai is big business. Sisterhood oversees a small kitchen located on the first floor and supervises any dairy food request for smaller parties. Sisterhood activities have always benefited the temple and any Sisterhood-catered event, from a small organizational meeting to a bar or bat mitzvah luncheon, essentially feeds Sinai's hungry coffers.

Sinai's Own Tastemaker: Murray Cohen

In 1968, Sinai expanded its culinary palate by hiring the now-legendary Murray Cohen through his company JEM Caterers. Murray, as *everyone* calls him, and his wife of 58 years, Millie, hail from Brooklyn, New York; they had their original catering business in the Five Towns area on Long Island. They came to Los Angeles with their three children—Steven, Michael, and Paula—all of whom have become kosher caterers in the Los Angeles and Las Vegas areas.

JEM Caterers is an independent company and Sinai Temple's official caterer. Murray has private clients who contract with him to cater their affairs on site at Sinai Temple. He has a financial arrangement with the temple whereby Sinai collects a percentage of his fee in exchange for allowing him to operate there. Murray does a tremendous amount of business: the money Sinai collects is quite significant and contributes greatly to the temple's budget.

JEM provides all nondairy victuals for all sorts of meetings and events. It also provides daily lunch for the children and staff at Sinai Akiba Academy. Murray likes trying out his new recipes on staffers.

The Sinai Temple kitchen is a strictly kosher facility and Nicholas Mermell, Sinai's ritual director for over 30 years and also a *mashgiach*, certifies its *kashrut* daily. The catering staff typically arrives at 7 A.M. to prepare for morning meetings and school lunch, and has stayed as late as 2 A.M. for parties.

Murray began his career as a butcher, but this didn't satisfy his strong creative streak that is evident to anyone who has attended any JEM-catered affair. Murray loves making people happy. Nothing pleases him more than pleasing others: he puts his own heart and soul into his work. He specializes in hors d'oeuvres that are so delicious that people often fill up before dinner is served. He was the first kosher caterer in Los Angeles to provide elegant French Service catering, meaning that trained servers carry artfully displayed trays of food to each table and serve each guest individually, according to their preferences.

To keep customers' costs down, Murray works in such high volume that he can command certain discounts from his suppliers. Still, kosher food is naturally expensive on the West Coast since there are no longer any kosher slaughterhouses for meat or for poultry west of Indianapolis, and everything must be ordered in advance and then shipped. Requesting organic chicken makes the price even higher because most of what little there is comes from Canada. When asked if there were one thing he hopes his clients know, he said, "They get high quality food that tastes delicious, and I'll do everything I can to make them happy!"

Nevertheless, as expected, someone always complains about something. Once, during a gala dinner, Harvey Powell, a dear friend of Murray's, complained that his portions were too small. Murray went into the kitchen, took an entire side of ribs, wedged it into a long, four-pound, oversized challah, and had servers carry the "sandwich" out to him on a huge platter. Without missing a beat, Mr. Powell picked it up and started eating it ... with a huge grin on his face!

The first Sinai kitchen Murray worked in was small by anyone's standards. He performed miracles for years, delivering magnificent meals from meager facilities. After it became apparent that a third phase of construction at Sinai would be necessary in the 1990s, Murray helped design a new kitchen, where his staff of six full-time chefs and five assistants works today.

The kitchen is enormous compared with 12th and Valencia's. If the founders of Sinai Temple were to see Murray's kitchen now, they would find a walk-in refrigerator and freezer, four sets of double-stacked ovens, three fryers, three stoves with burners, one large dishwasher, and settings for 700 people!

Additionally, Murray also contributes food or food services to numerous charities around Los Angeles, from baking challahs for prisoners, to donating food to local rabbis for distribution to the hungry, to supporting Camp Ramah's (disabled) Tikvah Kids, which he has done for over 20 years. Sinai Temple recognized the Cohens by honoring them with a dinner-dance in 1988. Of course, it was a JEM of an evening!

Sisterhood

The two major organizations that have traditionally defined Sinai Temple are Sisterhood and the Men's Club. Each is open to members and nonmembers, although only members may hold executive office. Both have a legacy of active participation in the well-being of the temple. But they differ in notable ways.

Sisterhood functions as a vital supplemental fundraising arm of the temple, with every activity supporting the synagogue's financial operation. Whether catering a dairy event, buying scrip to local companies, or purchasing items in the temple's gift shop, a woman's involvement in Sisterhood is a statement of solidarity with Sinai that helps underwrite the various temple activities.

Years ago, Sisterhood activities offered mostly nonworking women an opportunity to meet each other for social

Diane Miller (left) honored by the women's division for Israel bonds, and event chair, Shirley Kirsch.

entertainment, education, classes, and community service, and to express their organizational skills and creativity within a socially acceptable milieu. A number of its women distinguished themselves for their outstanding dedication, among them Augusta Kohn, Celia Aberman, Sally Brandes, and Shirley Kirsch.

Today, with most young women and many mothers working outside the home as well as in it, Sisterhood faces new challenges in making itself and its programs relevant to more time-challenged women. Hopefully, it will continue to offer them an outlet for friendship, a resource for networking professionally and within the Jewish community, and—most importantly—an opportunity for synagogue and community leadership development.

The Men's Club

The Men's Club of Sinai Temple (under the auspices of the Federation of Jewish Men's Clubs since 1950) has existed almost as long as the temple. Board minutes mention it as far back as 1931, when it was called Brotherhood and S. A. Miller was its president. For a short while, there was even a Young Men's Brotherhood with an age limit of 25, later raised to 28.

It never has been a fundraising organization by charter, but throughout its history, it has usually contributed something to the temple and also to the U.J. Mostly, the Men's Club operates as a social network for men with time devoted to a variety of causes, both at home and abroad. The Men's Club also sponsors picnics, basketball games, and barbeques as well as a softball team that participates in a Los Angeles area synagogue softball league. Phil Rosenbaum, manager of the softball team for the past ten years, is the only Men's Club president to serve a three-year term.

Whereas Sisterhood promotes activity within the temple, Men's Club tends to focus externally. It is partially through the Men's Club that Milt Hyman's dream of

commemorating Yom HaShoah has come to pass: each year, in addition to the sanctuary service, the Men's Club distributes thousands of yellow *yahrzeit* candles throughout the entire Jewish community as a reminder to never forget.

In fact, the Men's Club has helped Sinai Temple achieve renown throughout the United States and around the world. Any man wearing a bright red yarmulke—silk or suede—is, most likely, a Men's Club member. Sinai's chapter has produced two international presidents— Jules Porter and Sidney Katz—and it has brought distinction to the congregation through its annual Burning Bush dinners.

Originally conceived as intimate weeknight dinners that honored a hard-working club member, today the Burning Bush dinners have become gala black-tie fundraisers that honor a variety of men, women, and couples. Early on, the proceeds primarily supported the temple and UJ, with other local Jewish organizations also receiving help.

Today, thanks to the encouragement of David Matloob, proceeds go toward worthy causes in Israel. Jacob Melamed helped organize the purchase of fire trucks and ambulances that bear the name of Sinai Temple/Los Angeles on their sides, and food banks and other Israeli social service organizations also have benefited from Sinai's largesse. People in Israel know Sinai Temple without ever having been here: what they know is that it cares about more than just itself.

Programming

Sinai Temple has an enormous variety of programming to satisfy a diverse array of interests across a broad age spectrum, including everything from USY for high school youth to ATID, which provides activities for young singles and couples ages 21–39, to Dor Chadash, for families with young children, to the Chai Society, which focuses on the over-55 crowd. There are other groups, too, and collectively, they all make the temple an exciting place for activities every day of the week from early morning until 10 P.M. almost every night.

The Temple Grows

As the temple looked to grow, it found that SAA served as an effective tool to recruit new members with school-age children. If membership was required for enrollment, then it seemed logical that if a family joined, its children should be entitled to go there. But a lack of physical space and a dearth of teachers prohibited the schools from expanding in some relative proportion to the bulging application pool.

This did not sit well with parents. Twice as many children applied as could be accepted, and this had a deleterious effect when children were being turned away. Demand clearly existed, and SAA had the potential to mushroom into a seriously large operation: it behooved Sinai Temple to make room for its growing student population.

As an interim solution, the board decided to convert the Hall of the Builders at the front of the temple into classroom area for Sinai's smallest students since, by law, and for safety's sake, they may only be taught at ground-floor level. This freed up other valuable classroom space for older pupils. Without too much architectural modification, although at significant cost, the renovation occurred.

This crisis in classroom space prompted the temple to examine its future seriously. If Sinai ran out of space in the school, young families would no longer join. If that happened, the temple would face a grim reality. The board commissioned a demographic study to determine, as best it could, the future needs of the community. The data that came in supported its hunch: expansion was essential. But *where* could the temple grow?

Men's Club president, David Matloob, poses for a photo with the team.

Aside from needing additional space, the existing structure needed serious refurbishing. Kambiz Hekmat, one of the temple's members with experience in engineering, recommended the temple could economize by hiring an in-house engineer instead of subcontracting most of its work. His apt suggestion was well received and proved correct. By hiring Luis Martinez as head custodian, and Frank Fortin as building engineer, Mr. Hekmat brilliantly helped the temple save enormous sums of money right away.

Mr. Martinez became a beloved fixture himself within the halls of Sinai. When he retired a few years ago, the ever-happy Carlos Barillos, who had been with Sinai for almost ten years already, began looking after Wilshire and Beverly Glen by supervising the dependable and hardworking maintenance crew.

As for expanding, luckily, thanks to Ruth and Allen Ziegler, Sinai Temple finally owned the entire city block from Wilshire and Beverly Glen to Ashton and Holmby. All that would be required for its expansion would be to raze the existing structures on the property along the south side of the temple ... and then raise millions of dollars for a new building, and another building campaign took root.

Building Phase III—Barad Hall and The Preschool

Jan Zakowski spearheaded a 7-year development campaign to raise money to build the synagogue to its outermost property lines, primarily to expand the school to allow for more students. Gerald Burg, executive director, helped Mrs. Zakowski in this massive undertaking, and they worked together like a one–two punch, using their complementary skills and comprehensive business acumen to accomplish an almost superhuman task.

Once again, Dr. Kamenir masterfully supervised the construction, this time done by The Tishman Company. It involved working with eighteen different local neighborhood organizations and obtaining hard-won building variances and waivers that ultimately produced new school facilities for SAA, a new preschool facility, and a play yard. The school facilities are already too small ... happy testament to Sinai's healthy growth, but a recurring problem for accommodating future membership needs.

Phase III of Sinai's expansion also included Barad Hall, named for Jill and Tom Barad, beloved members of the Sinai Community. The city's largest synagogue ballroom can accommodate up to 600 people for a sit-down gala dinner or seat approximately 900 during the High Holidays as an additional sanctuary, which, fortunately, is more than adequate for Sinai's needs for many years to come.

Mount Sinai Memorial Park/Simi Valley

As Sinai Temple grew, so did Mount Sinai Memorial Park (MSMP) in Hollywood. In fact, it began to approach capacity as it serviced the needs of Sinai Temple and the rest of the Jewish community. The overriding issue for members of the cemetery management committee (CMC) concerned what to do when the cemetery reached capacity.

The elders of Sinai who originally purchased MSMP fundamentally believed in the sanctity of providing Jews with dignified and kosher burial, and they passed this sacred commitment to the next generation of *shomrim*, guardians, on the CMC. The decision was made to find more land to build a second memorial park that would secure a holy place for Jewish burial well into the 22nd century.

For the next ten years, Dr. Kamenir diligently searched for suitable property that met the various requirements for development as a cemetery. He finally found an enormous area of undeveloped land in Simi Valley—180 acres altogether, divided into six separate, adjoining lots, only two of which were for cemetery use. Sinai Temple bought the land and then Dr. Kamenir astutely negotiated the resale of two of those six parcels to others. Unusable land was gifted to the city. With the purchase price nearly covered by the planned sell-off of the rezoned acreage, Dr. Kamenir practically guaranteed the temple's future financial security through MSMP/Simi Valley, based on future sales at the park.

For all of Dr. Kamenir's far-reaching vision—including supervision of building Phases II and III of the Wilshire and Beverly Glen facility, and the entire development of MSMP/Simi Valley (to name just some of his contributions to Sinai Temple for over 50 years)—Sinai Temple honored him and his wife by naming the Simi chapel in their honor.

Reception; Dr. Eric Ray seated.

Mount Sinai Memorial Park Simi Valley captures a unique and compelling harmony between the land and the architecture.

It is a glorious, light-filled space that surpasses in size and beauty some of the finest modern sanctuaries of worship. Seven stained glass windows designed by temple member Ruth Merritt adorn the ceiling line of the chapel's back wall. That this sanctuary happens to be located within a memorial park is not a fluke. It serves as a living legacy to the beauty of life, the same destination for us all, and the Jewish commitment to dignity throughout the journey.

The 90th Anniversary of Sinai

By the time Sinai Temple celebrated its 90th anniversary in 1996, during Judy Galperson's term of office, there was much cause to celebrate. First and foremost, the temple still existed. It had survived scandals, setbacks, financial woes, and personality conflicts. Nothing seemed capable of breaking the determination instilled by the original founders. As Jews are fond of saying, "Thank God!"

Using the 90th anniversary as impetus to begin preparing for the centennial, Soraya Nazarian and Howard Brandes together began to assemble a huge array of photos and documents that help tell the story of the temple. Without their foresight and initial efforts to preserve materials, invaluable historical records might have been lost. Much of this book would not have been possible without the "seeds" for an archive they planted. Mr. Brandes probably knows more encyclopedic detail about Sinai's history than almost any other member today, and he is enthusiastic and willing to share such information with anyone interested.

The highlight of the 90th anniversary (the 90th Anniversary Committee was chaired by Tom Barad) was the commission of a new *sefer* Torah for the congregation. Dr. Eric Ray, a well-known artist, acted as *sofer* (scribe) and came to Los Angeles from Israel four times over the course of the year. Every Torah is special, and this one is particularly so, because so many people helped bring it to life.

Unfortunately, there was a cloud over the celebration. Shortly before, Rabbi Schranz had announced his departure. Several years earlier, he had undergone coronary bypass surgery to prevent a future heart attack. His recovery lasted several months at home. During his short-term absence, either he, or the congregation, or maybe both, had a metaphoric "change of heart," and rabbi and flock began to drift apart.

Nearly 400 family members had resigned over a period of about two years, posing a serious threat to the economic health of the temple. The issue was compounded by the fact that for all the members who had grown dissatisfied with the rabbi's performance, there were an equal number of congregants whose admiration and affection for him had grown exponentially.

Inevitably, something had to be done. The board considered not renewing the rabbi's contract when it next expired—in about eighteen months—but that was a long time to expect a divided and dwindling congregation to wait for resolution.

It seemed no one would be completely satisfied, but the board did its best to come up with a Solomonic solution. Contractually, the rabbi was entitled to a 6-month sabbatical after he served Sinai for a period of seven years. Rabbi Schranz already had been at Sinai for eight and a half years. If he took his sabbatical, then only twelve months remained on his current contract.

The board encouraged him to take his paid sabbatical, and then offered to buy out his last year, giving him the title "Emeritus," but asking no responsibilities of him. He accepted this proposal. Sinai's board did what it believed was in the best interests of the temple, and, as had been the case when Rabbi Silverman left, the congregation was traumatized for quite some time.

Immediately after he left, the rabbi received a position at the Ziegler School for Rabbinic Studies at the UJ for a year. Following that, Sutton Place Synagogue in New York City hired him, and he has remained there ever since. His congregation loves him and theirs seems to be a match made in heaven.

Thirteen: A Very Special Number

For the thirteenth time in nearly a century, Sinai Temple needed a new rabbi.

Rabbi David Wolpe.

Chapter Thirteen

Forward in Faith

Rabbi David Wolpe of fourth-floor High Holiday renown, had been affiliated with Sinai Temple since 1983. Young, enthusiastic, extremely bright, and energetic, he knew members of the interview committee and even the names of their kids. Author of a much-admired first book, *The Healer of Shattered Hearts*, the Rabbi dazzled everyone he met. In 1997, Sinai proudly hired Rabbi Wolpe to escort it out of the 20th century and into the 21st.

David Wolpe never aspired to be a pulpit rabbi. Studious and scholarly, he would have been happy to surround himself with books, filling his days with serious thought about deep issues.

As the rabbi of an enormous congregation, he does just that. Each member is like a living book with a unique story that describes, in one way or another, a variety of the deepest issues imaginable: life and death, pain and suffering, honor and glory, hope and redemption. Rabbi Wolpe gets to consider all these themes as they apply and play out in modern Jewish life.

Born on September 19, 1958, in Harrisburg, Pennsylvania, David Wolpe was one of four sons of the distinguished Rabbi Gerald and Elaine Wolpe. A 1981 graduate of the University of Pennsylvania and ordained through JTS in 1987, he was already familiar with Los Angeles, having studied at the UJ from 1982–1984, followed by teaching there (and, later, at JTS, Hunter College in New York City, and UCLA), and serving as the UJ's library director.

While at the UJ, the rabbi also met his future wife, Eileen Ansel. They married in 1992 and moved back East in 1995, where Rabbi Wolpe assisted Chancellor Ismar Schorsch at the Seminary. He also continued teaching, guest lecturing around the country, and contributing to numerous publications writing articles and reviews. Since then, Rabbi Wolpe has firmly secured his place in Jewish literature by authoring five more critically acclaimed books, including the 1999 national best seller *Making Loss Matter: Creating Meaning in Difficult Times*, in addition to writing a weekly column for syndication in various Jewish newspapers.

Rabbi Wolpe claimed the senior rabbi position of one of the largest and most high-profile Conservative synagogues in the country at the youthful age of 38. His wife had recently given birth to their first child, Samara, and they were excited to start a family together and join the Sinai "family." Accepting the job at Sinai was a huge step for the rabbi because it forced him out of his comfort zone.

Not long after he began, Mrs. Wolpe was diagnosed with an aggressive form of cervical cancer, which necessitated aggressive medical intervention. An ancient Jewish custom calls for changing one's name during, or immediately after, a life-threatening illness in order to confuse and keep away the Angel of Death. Mrs. Wolpe embraced this tradition and changed her first name to Eliana, which means "My God Has Answered Me." Fortunately, Mrs. Wolpe (often affectionately called "Elli") survived and was, in time, restored to health, allowing her to resume the challenges of, and blessings from, supporting her husband and rearing their daughter together.

Mrs. Wolpe has a master's degree from the UJ in business administration for nonprofit organizations. She is a welcome presence whenever she attends classes at Sinai because she contributes insightful commentary, especially when she joins Rabbi Wolpe's weekly morning Torah class. The two of them clearly have fun together. In addition, on her own, she has become highly knowledgeable in the areas of macrobiotic nutrition and alternative health, with a special interest in toxicity and the environment.

The long hours and unpredictable schedule of being a pulpit rabbi can make family life difficult. Crises and funerals (to name but a few reasons) necessitate frequent schedule changes which make any normal routine nearly impossible. One of Rabbi Wolpe's greatest challenges is to adhere to a strict schedule in his office and establish clear time boundaries outside so he can carve out private time for himself and his family.

Making SAA the Best School Possible

Sinai Temple recognized in the early 1990s that it would need to upgrade soon and physically expand Sinai Akiba Academy to keep up with a growing student population and continue providing its own children with state-of-the-art education and facilities. By 1997, Phase III of the synagogue's build-out was complete. In addition to spacious Barad Hall, the school transitioned into a brand-new building, with beautiful classrooms and even a second gym, donated by Laurence and Barbi Weinberg. Their daughter, Jan Zakowski, ably led Sinai as president during the development campaign with her devotion for building for future generations.

The Douglas Family Early Childhood Center

The expansion also made room for the Douglas Family Early Childhood Center (DFECC), which provides an excellent foundation for developing minds and nurturing tender souls. Actor Kirk Douglas experienced newfound meaning in Judaism in his later life, and in addition to becoming an adult bar mitzvah and renewing his wedding vows (with Rabbi Wolpe officiating), he and his wife, Anne, endowed the preschool. Mr. Douglas emphatically believes in supporting the temple. He even extolled, in his 2003 Kol Nidre Appeal, the virtues of spending one's children's inheritance instead of giving it to them: "Our temple is doing a wonderful job with our children as well as adults. It has done a lot for me. The 'kids' won't mind. Let's help the Sinai Temple."

The DFECC offers a happy place for preschoolers, from age two-years-and-four months through kindergarten. Children play with other children in a bright and cheerful environment and learn everything from colors and numbers to sharing and caring. Teachers give them a rudimentary experience of the Jewish holidays and they learn that being Jewish is special and fun. The teachers all have the highest credentials for working with youngsters; SAA's headmaster, Rabbi Scheindlin, supervises the school's curriculum.

Sinai Temple Religious School

Congregation Sinai's first school was its religious school. From its earliest days, the temple and its members sought to instill a solid Jewish education in youngsters. The school's format has changed over the years to reflect the membership's needs. At various times, it has been an every-day-after-secular-school school; sometimes, three days per week; at times, two ... and sometimes *only* a Sunday school! Its overall mandate has never changed, however: to teach Hebrew and to provide Sinai youth with Judaic education and religious training.

Recently, Sinai Temple Religious School adopted the acronym ST*RS. Prior to the temple's absorption of Akiba Academy (which gave it its own on-site Jewish day school), the religious school served as the primary focus of Jewish education for Sinai's children. Since many Sinai children now attend SAA and receive a significant portion of their Hebrew and Jewish education there as part of the regular curriculum, the religious school has lost some of its draw. But for those members' children who attend other primary and middle schools, the religious school offers first-rate Hebrew language study and a full menu of bible study and Judaic instruction necessary to become bar or bat mitzvah and to be on a par with all other Jewish children in the Conservative movement.

Parents sending their children to ST*RS have every reason to be confident in the school and proud of their children's achievements.

More (and More and More) Rabbis

By this time, Rabbi Emeritus Dershowitz, still an excellent support, no longer worked full time. Therefore, in the fall of 1998, Sinai needed someone special to lead Barad Hall High Holiday Services. Sinai turned to Rabbi Bradley Shavit Artson, who had graduated Harvard College in 1981 and had been ordained by the Jewish Theological Seminary with honors in 1988. For the past ten years, he had been rabbi of a Congregation in Mission Viejo, which greatly expanded under his tenure. In the years that Rabbi Artson has annually conducted Barad Hall services, he has become vice president of the UJ and later Dean of the Ziegler School of Rabbinic Studies, where the student population more than doubled under his leadership. He also became the Executive Director of the Board of Rabbis of Southern California.

Through his introduction to Judaism program, he helped over 200 people convert to Judaism. In 2006, the Federation of Jewish Men's Clubs honored Rabbi Artson with the Red

Religious school Bet Siddur dedication. Top row, left to right: Assistant to the Director, Sharon Berman and Director of Education, Aviva Leibovitz.

Yarmulka Humanitarian Award, to benefit the Ziegler School's Student Scholarship Fund. The celebration was held at Sinai Temple.

Not long after Rabbi Wolpe started, the magnitude of his workload (by virtue of Sinai being so large) made it clear to him that he should seek an associate. A search began for another rabbi, but the very size of the congregation dictated and restricted who could interview for the position.

The Rabbinical Assembly (RA) of America categorizes Conservative congregations according to their membership size. It also differentiates among rabbis' seniority based on the number of years since their ordination, as well as the size of congregation(s) they already have experience leading. The RA considers Sinai a very large congregation, which mandates that its senior rabbi have at least ten years' previous experience in the field.

Rabbi Wolpe did have the ten years required, although he hadn't spent them working as a pulpit rabbi. Nevertheless, he was well known and respected, and the congregation aggressively recruited him, so the RA permitted the *shul* to make him its offer. Assistant and associate rabbis don't need so much prior experience, but everyone assumed the RA would highly scrutinize the next rabbi to be brought on board ... especially since the search took place only one year later.

One might surmise that Rabbi Wolpe would propose someone with significant experience and who would fulfill a laundry list of RA qualifications. To the contrary, both the Wolpes knew a wonderful person just recently out of rabbinic school, but with all the essential qualifications nonetheless, and Mrs. Wolpe emphatically asserted that this candidate was right for Sinai. Being a smart Jewish husband, Rabbi Wolpe listened to her: he recommended his "protégée" to the search committee, and this is how Rabbi Sherre Zwelling (who later married and became Rabbi Hirsch) came to Sinai in 1998 ... brainy, beautiful, respectful of tradition, and replete with new ideas.

Rabbi Sherre Zwelling Hirsch

Rabbi Sherre Zwelling Hirsch wanted to be either a doctor or a rabbi. She felt she could make more of a difference in the world, and be a more meaningful role model for other women, however, as a female rabbi than as a female physician. Moreover, she truly felt a calling to serve God and humankind. After graduating from Northwestern University in 1991 with honors in American culture, she

Our first female Rabbi with three past Sisterhood Presidents: Left to right: Judy Fisher, Jina Rezvanpour, Rabbi Hirsch, Brina Rosenbaum.

began what would be a slightly circuitous route to becoming a rabbi.

Starting at the UJ, she received her first master's degree in rabbinics, but then left the program, uncertain about becoming a rabbi. A few years later, following additional studies in Jerusalem, she reenrolled at JTS, fully committed to her career path. She graduated in 1998 and came to Sinai shortly after, at the age of 29.

Rabbi Zwelling brought a great deal of attention to Sinai Temple, primarily because she was its first female rabbi and because most women who become rabbis (about 30 percent of JTS students are female) do not opt for pulpit positions: the lack of control over one's time almost precludes any private life (as Rabbi Wolpe quickly discovered), and it definitely would infringe, to some degree, upon the ability to have or raise a family. But Rabbi Zwelling was still single, so it wasn't an immediate issue. Personable, gregarious, and an anomaly (as a female pulpit rabbi), many people came, at first, just to see her. She quickly displayed a talent for connecting with her peers, young couples, and families—and many of those who came to observe stayed.

Rabbi Wolpe encouraged Rabbi Zwelling to create a niche for herself working with those congregants who so easily related to her. In so doing, she made a very large synagogue seem quite intimate for a large number of people. Essentially, she took a city and made it into a village—and then many villages—with a variety of smaller, regular services tailored for folks with similar interests: "Torah in the Round," "Tot Shabbat," and "interactive" High Holiday services, where Rabbi Zwelling engaged in in-service dialogue with congregants to make sure everyone understood the prayers, their purpose, and meaning.

In 2000, Rabbi Zwelling married Dr. Jeffrey Hirsch, and their family now numbers five, with a son and two daughters. In early 2006, she announced her decision to leave Sinai in order to explore new and exciting opportunities. Rabbi Hirsch worked hard to balance the requirements of a pulpit rabbi with the requirements of a wife and mother.

Over the course of eight highly productive years, Rabbi Hirsch proved her mettle and made important and significant contributions at Sinai Temple, and throughout Los Angeles. In Argentina, she raised awareness and funds to support the South American Jewish community. She will remain in Los Angeles and active in the Jewish community, and fortunate will be those people whose lives she touches. Sinai Temple will miss her warmth, humor, and *Yiddishkeit*.

Rabbi Brian Schuldenfrei

Within a few years of Rabbi Hirsch's arrival, it became apparent that Rabbis Wolpe and Hirsch *together* could still not comfortably handle all the work that such an enormous *shul* generated. To remedy this, Sinai Temple engaged associate rabbi Mark Fasman (currently a rabbi in St. Louis), and a series of rabbinic interns, to help. In 2003, Rabbi Brian Schuldenfrei came to Sinai to fill the associate role and, to everyone's delight, he has just renewed his contract for another three years. With Rabbi Wolpe's blessing, he, too, like Rabbi Hirsch, has created a niche for himself: working with young people. He supervises the religious school director and oversees the ATID program (young adults, ages 21–39).

ATID, which means "future" in Hebrew, has a flagship program called the Ted and Hedy Orden and Family Friday Night Live (FNL) that regularly attracts over 1,000 people on the second Shabbat of the month. Rabbi Wolpe introduced the contemporary evening service shortly after he joined Sinai. With a grant from the Jewish Community Foundation and support from Ruth and Sid Pilot, Rose and Alex Farkas, and subsequently the Orden Family, it has been wildly embraced by the young Jewish community, and greatly emulated around the country. Craig Taubman and an ever-changing group of musicians fill the sanctuary with sacred music that rises to the heights of the ceiling and carries the spirit of inspired worshippers directly to the Divine.

Many young singles who have attended FNL say their prayers really were answered. For some, this means meeting their *bashert*, their intended. Numerous marriages have resulted from introductions through FNL. For others, answered prayer refers to reconnection with Judaism and a renewed interest in living a Jewish life. Regardless of the reasons for attending, after services end, Sinai Temple literally buzzes with energy. Israeli dancing usually takes place in one room, a guest speaker will lecture in Kohn Chapel, and people meet and greet one another in Gold and Traub Halls—the physical "heart" of the first floor.

Rabbi Schuldenfrei shares much in common with some of the FNL constituents. He was raised in a Reform Jewish home (and attended Temple Sinai in Cedarhurst on Long Island, New York) and says he really "stumbled across Judaism" after college. Overwhelmed by the richness of its tradition, coupled with his own passion for people, he decided to become a rabbi. He finds his life's meaning acting as a matchmaker to help forge relationships between Jewish people and their tradition. Once he helps awaken someone's identity and interest, he works hard through outreach to nurture that person's religious intellect and spirit to inspire long-term commitment.

To demonstrate Sinai's commitment to the FNL crowd, and in the hope of enticing more young people to join the temple, the board of directors—under the leadership of its president, Brina Rosenbaum—made two important decisions in 2003 at the first of three board retreats during her term. First, it asked Rabbi Schuldenfrei to reinstitute High Holiday services in Rickles Gym. Second, the board opened the services to young singles and married couples at a reduced membership rate (as it had done in the past) so they would really know that they and Sinai belonged to each other.

The first Friday Night Live Executive Committee 1998–1999. Standing: Jodi Berman, Vicky Asher, Dr. Deborah Rosenbaum. Seated: Rafi Abrishami and Cantor Paul Dorman.

These services were hugely popular when Rabbi Wolpe originally conducted them, and the temple hoped to duplicate the magic. Based on the standing-room-only crowd over the last few years, it's fair to say Rabbi Schuldenfrei has woven his own spell.

Like Rabbi Hirsch, Rabbi Schuldenfrei is impressed by Rabbi Wolpe's support of supplementary *minyanim* within Sinai Temple that appeal to a variety of congregants. His own style differs greatly from Rabbi Wolpe's and also Rabbi Hirsch's, and he considers himself fortunate to have the benefit of their combined experience, along with Rabbi Wolpe's regular critiques of his sermons.

Rabbi Schuldenfrei recently married Rabbi Deborah Bock, who was ordained through the Hebrew Union College.

A Persian President

While not every president has been identified by name in this book, each one has played a vital role in the congregation's history and development. With nearly 300 employees today and an annual operating budget of over $14,000,000, simply keeping the temple afloat is an enormous accomplishment for which every president deserves thanks and praise.

Some presidents have had to deal with extraordinary circumstances during their terms. One particular president didn't have an extraordinary circumstance: his entire life has been extraordinary. Jimmy Jamshid Delshad came to America with his brother at the age of 19, well before the 1979 revolution in Iran. He worked hard to put himself through UCLA and to become a successful businessman. He and his wife, Lonnie, joined Sinai Temple around 1973 and both became active.

As history has shown, the temple had a huge influx of Persian Jews after the Iranian revolution, and the temple did not initially welcome them as warmly as they deserved. It took many years for the major-

Hedy and Ted Orden and family, sponsors of Friday Night Live, celebrate their extraordinary torah.

ity Ashkenazi members to accept their Middle Eastern co-religionists who brought with them different language and traditions. In spite of the factionalism, in 1999, Mr. Delshad decided to run for president of the congregation. Even his beloved father-in-law thought he couldn't win.

To most everyone's surprise, the board voted him in. It was a bold move, fraught with huge implications. For himself, he had to achieve great things. If he did, it would open the door for other Persians in the congregation to seek other leadership roles.

Effecting any sort of change within a large organization is akin to steering an ocean liner. It moves in very, very small increments. Change takes place much more slowly than one might imagine or desire. Mr. Delshad did an admirable job running the ship and keeping it on a good course. He set a positive tone for Persian members of the congregation to do whatever their hearts desired at Sinai. Mr. Delshad was recently elected Vice Mayor of the City of Beverly Hills, again proving that anything is possible in America with hard work and determination.

While steering as captain of the Sinai ship, Mr. Delshad navigated it straight to the Ocean of Wisdom. The name Dalai Lama translates as Ocean of

Wisdom, and His Holiness visited the temple in 1999 as part of the World Festival of Sacred Music. Sinai Temple historically has used music to transcend words and bring worlds together. In this case, it linked the spiritual leader of the Tibetan people in exile to all Jews living in the Diaspora, and in the case of Sinai Temple, to Persian Jews similarly living in exile.

Cantor David Silverstein

Sinai's own Cantor David Silverstein helped orchestrate the Dalai Lama's visit. A fourth-generation Sinai-ite, Cantor Silverstein (pronounced Silver-styne) was raised at Sinai, studied under Cantor Urstein, and joined the temple in 1993 as a second full-time cantor in addition to Meir Finkelstein. For a while, it seemed like having a name that ended in "steen" or "styne" was a prerequisite to being a part of Sinai's musical staff!

Then, in the mid-1990s, Cantor Finkelstein decided to give up singing for a career in retail. He tried it briefly, but then changed his mind and returned to Sinai full time. Sinai was thrilled to still have him, but he eventually left in 1996 when he moved to Texas.

Just as timing and luck played an important role in the development of Rabbi Artson's career at Sinai, so, too, did they probably affect Cantor Silverstein's. When the cantorial position opened up, many people assumed that Cantor Silverstein would automatically fill it. But many other people in the congregation still remembered Cantor Gole and wanted him to come back. At the same time, the executive director of the temple left and that position also needed filling.

After holding auditions for the cantor, the board rehired Cantor Gole. But it could not find an executive director as easily—and everyone liked and trusted Cantor Silverstein—so the temple offered and he accepted the position as interim executive director until he found another pulpit for himself. To this day, Cantor Silverstein is still, and always will be, a beloved son of Sinai. He serves as cantor of new Temple Israel of San Antonio, Texas. In a spirit of friendship and typical cooperation, he helpfully contributed toward the creation of this book by sharing memories and memorabilia.

Cantor Joseph Gole: The Encore

Cantor Gole returned in 2000, bringing with him not only his beautiful voice, but also a spiritual depth that comes with maturity. In perfect counterpoint to his previous uncertainty about being a full-time cantor, he rejoined the congregation

His Holiness, the fourteenth Dalai Lama, is escorted to the bimah by Cantor David Silverstein.

exuding not just confidence in his talent, but also conviction in his purpose.

A huge part of that purpose is to use music as a timeless bridge that links people together in the here-and-now, as well as to our ancestors through the centuries. Cantor Gole wants to help people experience the holiness of Judaism through sound. It is significant that he came back to Sinai after an 18-year hiatus. He is full of life and invests his reverence for it into everything he does, from chanting the priestly blessings at a bar or bat mitzvah, to singing "*El Molay Rachamim*" at a funeral.

Through his voice, the cantor soulfully conveys his own sense of wonder about the miracle and constancy of God's love and the continuity of that message through music. He prides himself on "being there" for congregants in need and believes that this quality of presence and attention is, perhaps, his greatest contribution to the congregation. In 2006, Sinai Temple hired Arianne Brown as Cantor Sheni. Both she and Cantor Gole will work with choir director and organist Aryell Cohen.

Howard Lesner

Another person who is "always there" at and for Sinai is its current executive director, Howard Lesner. The son of Mickey and Dr. Julius Lesner (the former Sinai director of education), Howard Lesner practically grew up at Sinai and literally knows every inch of it. (He used to play hide-and-seek in the ceiling above Ziegler Hall before its completion.) Today, he runs the temple, doing everything from implementing the budget to overseeing the employees to making sure the air conditioning and elevators run. Mr. Lesner believes it is *bashert* that he works at Sinai since it is like a second home and family to him. He spends more waking hours here than anywhere else.

Knowing the building as well as he does, and loving it as much, Mr. Lesner noticed physical deterioration when he started working here. Knowing, further, that people are more apt to support something they're proud of, he understood the need to make Sinai look as good as possible. He worked with then–president Mr. Delshad to convince the board to allocate $500,000 for a gentle facelift for a building in use seven days a week. New carpeting, lighting, and outside painting helped restore Sinai's luster, and Mr. Lesner has seen to it that the temple is properly maintained ever since.

Good looks definitely matter, but safety comes first. Perhaps one of the greatest contributions toward Sinai's well-being was the hiring of Colin Webb by Gerry Burg to oversee all security. Mr. Webb supervises security officers at the temple. He understands the importance of keeping sharp eyes and well-tuned ears to everything that happens on site. In addition, he is responsible for overseeing security during the High Holidays and coordinating with outside security when major dignitaries—such as the late Israeli Prime Minister Yitzhak Rabin or Los Angeles Mayor Antonio Villaraigosa—visit.

Every executive director works closely with each president to make sure the board's approved programs are implemented properly, carried out within budget, and completed on time. Abner Goldstine, a past president and currently the associate centennial campaign chair, makes regular stops in Mr. Lesner's office and, with current president Tom Flesh, skillfully keeps lines of communication open and flowing.

The Centennial President, Robert Thomas Flesh

President Tom Flesh has had the privilege of guiding the temple leading up to and during its centennial year. He is the public face of the synagogue at Shabbat services and within the Jewish and secular communities. Both Mr. Flesh's family and his wife Judy's family have been longtime members of the temple: Tom's leadership is a natural progression of next-generation commitment and volunteerism.

He brings to this job great personal warmth and some rather unique business and political skills that few others possess. In addition to being an attorney and successful entrepreneur, he has been president of the Motor Vehicle Board for the State of California, chair of the Sheriff's Youth Foundation under Sheriff Lee Baca, and on the board of the Los Angeles Police Reserves, and a member of the Board of Councilors, University of Southern California. Friendly and caring, he is dedicated to securing Sinai's place in history for many generations to come.

100 and Beyond

For its centennial celebration, Sinai Temple planned several memorable events and activities. In addition to Professor Elie Wiesel coming to the temple as a scholar-in-residence, there was a formal dedication of the Ziegler sanctuary on Shavuot, a gala afternoon musical concert on June 4, 2006, with entertainment for the entire family, and a gourmet dinner-dance that evening at the Beverly Hilton Hotel. Celebrity chefs from around the world prepared "an epicurean evening of biblical delights." In addition, the centennial committee asked Penny Dain, Public Relations Coordinator, to design a keepsake family photo album that incorporated pictures of Sinai members from the first hundred years.

As the temple passes this milestone, it cannot rest on its laurels. Every day brings a new challenge. This fact was never clearer than in 2003, when 45-year-old Rabbi Wolpe suffered a grand mal seizure while attending a Hillel dedication ceremony in Philadelphia at the University of Pennsylvania. Good friends and fellow alumni Marc and Julie Platt, and Irwin and Helgard Field (Mrs. Platt and Mr. Field co-chaired the centennial committee) helped Rabbi Wolpe return to Los Angeles, where doctors determined he had

Ruth and Sidney Pilot honored for their many kind deeds.

a brain lesion. For almost two weeks, the temple hovered at the edge of the unknown, in the hands of the Almighty, with its rabbi "blessed with everything." ("*V'Hashem Baruch Et Avraham Bakol*" ... "God blessed Abraham with everything.") When a complete diagnosis was made, it was benign.

This event gave everyone an unexpected opportunity to do what the rabbi does regularly—think deep thoughts about important things. Certainly, everyone thought about Sinai's singular leader and prayed fervently for his *refuah sh'lema*. It did not go unnoticed among those who had been at Sinai since he started that a dark cloud seemed to hang over his family's health. Everyone was scared—scared for his life, for his wife and child, and selfishly, but understandably, scared for themselves and the future of the temple.

Would the rabbi survive? Would he recover completely? After all, it was brain surgery. Would he be able to return to work, and would he still be the same Rabbi Wolpe everyone knew? And if not, what then? During what were truly days of awe, temple staff and lay leadership did an exceptional job under extraordinary pressure to keep the congregation informed and as upbeat as possible.

As we know now, everything (thank God) turned out well, the rabbi was restored to health, and after a private recovery at home over several months, he returned to his Sinai "family." Rabbi Wolpe acknowledged his own brush with mortality not by changing his name but by performing a specific *mitzvah* written in the Torah: he commissioned the writing of a *sefer* Torah in gratitude for his salvation.

Sinai Temple
cordially invites you and your family
to participate in the
Dedication Ceremony
of the
Ruth & Allen Ziegler
Sanctuary
Shavuot, Friday, June 2, 2006
in the Sanctuary 8:45 a.m.

Followed by a luncheon
honoring
Ruth Ziegler
immediately following Services
in Barad Hall
featuring the Worldwide Orchestra
led by Zade

Rabbi David Wolpe, Chair   Michael Nazarian, Co-chair

The congregation was overjoyed to have their rabbi back and helped underwrite "The Second Chance Torah"—in tribute to all who are lucky to receive a "second chance" and in honor of Rabbi Wolpe, a man who interprets the Torah's ancient, timeless words for all who seek to gain wisdom, and who uses language so skillfully to enrich the modern world in which we live.

Rabbi Wolpe doesn't have the gift of gab—small talk is not for him—but he is a highly gifted orator. He combines a love of English literature and perfect command of the Hebrew language with his own sensitivity and insight into human nature to produce powerful, weekly sermons. They teach, inspire, enlighten, challenge and otherwise invite people to examine, with fresh eyes and an open mind, things they already *thought* they knew about. This is in addition to a regular caseload of correspondence, commentary, counseling, a syndicated column, and performing life cycle events, among all his other work. No wonder he keeps impromptu conversation to a minimum!

Rabbi Wolpe's other hallmark talent, which came almost as a surprise to him, but which is essential for every sizable organization, is his ability to successfully fundraise on behalf of the temple and on behalf of Jews, locally and worldwide. Rabbi Kohn started a Sinai tradition of notable philanthropy by soliciting on behalf of Israel Bonds and the UJ. Rabbi Silverman picked up where he left off and Rabbi Wolpe is well on his way to surpassing Rabbi Silverman's fundraising legacy. Publicly, he uses his gifted way with words to raise general consciousness through his extraordinary sermons. Privately, he speaks to individuals and small groups of movers-and-shakers to raise cause-specific awareness and solicit funds needed to help those causes.

The torah was carried home from Israel in this duffel bag.

Whether it is for a development initiative at Sinai or for Israel Bonds or to help stop genocide in Darfur, Rabbi Wolpe speaks from his heart and uses his best persuasive powers to promote what he believes in. With the skill of a statesman, he lays out a nearly unassailable argument for philosophical support, followed by a compelling argument for financial support as well. By helping people understand their own role in *tikkun olam*, healing the world, he empowers them to become agents of real change. The money they contribute is, hopefully, just a first outer sign of inner growth and renewed purpose.

The temple recently embarked on a $36,000,000 capital campaign to cover costs for future development and advancement. Securing adequate funding will be critical to attain the goals the temple has set. These goals reflect the rabbi's vision for the future of Sinai Temple, which is being broadly referred to as "Sinai: A Center for Jewish Life and Learning." With funds raised through the centennial campaign and beyond, the ultimate goal is to create a center dedicated to excellence in religious, educational, and social programming with a clear focus on Jewish values. This concept mirrors, to a great degree, the structure and purpose of Jewish Community Centers (JCC) here in the United States.

JCCs provide a central location for socialization, education, entertainment, sports and recreation, and social services all within a Jewish context. Children, youth, men, women, and seniors experience meaningful Jewish living, learning, and expression through relationship with other Jewish members in their own community.

Harmonious relationship with one another in a Jewish environment stems from the inherent relationship a Jewish "house" has with God, and it sets the stage for more conscious and enhanced relationship with people outside our immediate environment, throughout the rest of the world.

This three-way relationship reflects Rabbi Wolpe's concept of Conservative Judaism as "Covenantal Judaism." He originally voiced this view at the Jewish Theological Seminary in New York in early November 2005, in a lecture about the future of Conservative Judaism. According to Rabbi Wolpe, Covenantal Judaism is the Judaism of relationship.

Rabbi Wolpe and Sofer Yehuda Weill.

Jews live in relationship with God, with other Jews, and with all peoples and humanity.

God's covenant with Noah was to never again destroy the earth, and He gave Noah a rainbow for a sign. Rabbi Wolpe believes the shimmering half-circle of colored light must be completed by our own promise not to destroy each other and the world in which we live.

Conclusion

Sinai Temple has reached its centennial milestone surviving and thriving for 100 years. This magnificent synagogue and its vibrant, diverse congregation stands as a legacy of a small group of immigrants 100 years ago who desired to pray together—with their families bytheir sides—truly a miracle. And to live in a land of freedom where we can daily pray without fear for our lives is a blessing beyond all measure. Whether we say thank you, *toda rabah, gracias, merci,* or *motshakerem*, we have reason to be filled with gratitude.

But ancient wisdom tells us, "You should live until a hundred and twenty." Getting to this point is not enough. There is more to come. The journey is long. And the Promised Land yet awaits us. Sinai Temple crosses the threshold from today into tomorrow by embarking on the next leg of its journey to promote Jewish life, learning, and loving expression in freedom and peace.

The glory of its first 100 years will be relevant only in context of the story of its next. Being 100 is not so important as getting to 120, or 150, or 200. And therein lies the challenge. The Center for Jewish Life and Learning will succeed if it truly reflects not only the rabbi's vision, but also where the congregants of Sinai Temple want to go.

In a place like Los Angeles, where urban sprawl is the order of the day and isolation can occur without effort, it is wise to build a Jewish refuge against physical separation and spiritual alienation. Jews are indeed, and always have been, defined by our sense of community and, also, our understanding that we must actively nurture that community and each member of it.

Architect Eisenshtat's tent-like sanctuary, designed as an oasis in the midst of the city, must offer more than coffee and cushion to those who make their way to Wilshire and Beverly Glen. It should vouchsafe a well of spiritual restoration to refresh the weak and weary and give guidance to all on the road to Jerusalem. "How goodly are thy tents, O Jacob, thy dwellings, O Israel!"

It is only through vigilance that any endeavor survives. But it is only with joyous faith in the Almighty that the Jewish people thrives. May Sinai Temple flourish in the days that lie ahead, recalling its past for the lessons it can learn, embracing with courage and optimism what change the future must bring. We turn to each other for strength, support, and encouragement, in good times and in bad, from generation to generation.

"So teach us to number our days that we may get us a heart of wisdom."

A prayer of Moses, the man of God
Psalm 90, verse 12

Appendixes

Appendix One: Rabbis, Cantors, Choir Directors, and Organists of Sinai Temple (as of July 2006)

Rabbi/Assistant(s):*	*Years:*	*Cantor:*	*Years:*
Isidore Myers	1906-12	M. Katz	1905-09
		Moses Alter	1909-15
Rudolph Farber	1912-15	Jacob Weinstock	1915-18
David Liknaitz	1915-17	Jacob Weinstock	
Moses Rosenthal	1918-22	Abraham Silverman	1918-40
Mayer Winkler	1922-29	Abraham Silverman	
Max Kert	1929-30	Abraham Silverman	
Jacob Kohn	1931-52	Abraham Silverman	
Jacob Pressman	1947-50	Lieb Glantz	1941-46
David Lieber	1950-54	Carl Urstein	1947-72
Israel Chodos	1953-63	Carl Urstein	
Jacob Kohn (Emeritus)	1953-68		
Herbert D. Teitelbaum			
Julian White			
Daniel Merritt	1962-72		
Paul Dubin			
Max Vorspan (Westwood Community Methodist Church)			
Hillel Silverman	1964-80	Carl Urstein	
Jacob Kohn (Emeritus)		Joseph Gole	1972-82
Daniel Merritt			
Zvi Dershowitz	1972-		
Solomon Rothstein	1981-84	Joseph Gole	
Zvi Dershowitz		*Carl Urstein (Emeritus)*	
		Meir Finkelstein	1982-97
Moshe Tutnauer	1984-86	Meir Finkelstein	
Zvi Dershowitz			
Allan Schranz	1986-97	Meir Finkelstein	
Zvi Dershowitz		David Silverstein	
David Wolpe	1997-	Joseph Gole	2000-
Zvi Dershowitz (Emeritus)		Arianne Brown	2006-
Sherre Z. Hirsch	1998-2006		
Mark Fasman	1999-2002		
Brian Schuldenfrei	2003-		

Director:	*Years:*	*Choir Organist:***	*Years:*
		Eva Schauer	1926
		Roy Brignall	1937
		Roy Brignall	
		Lillian Klass	1941-46
		Maurice Goldman	1947-55
Alfred Sendry	1956-64		
		Max Helfman	1956-61
		Dr. Robt. Strassberg	
Erwin Jospe	1965-75		
Aryell Cohen	1974-	Aryell Cohen	1974-
Aryell Cohen		Aryell Cohen	
Aryell Cohen		Aryell Cohen	
Aryell Cohen		Aryell Cohen	

*Rabbis Teitelbaum and Merritt functioned primarily as directors of education. Others who filled that role were Rabbi Julian White, Paul Dubin, and Paul Schneider. Other rabbis and cantors functioned during High Holiday services at Sinai East, that is, at 4th and New Hampshire after the main congregation moved to Beverly Glen and Wilshire. This covered a period of about ten years.

**The current organ at Sinai Temple is a 14 Rank Robert Morton, Theatre Pipe Organ - combination pneumatic and digital. It was first installed in 1926 at 4th and New Hampshire. It was installed in 1960 at 10400 Wilshire Blvd.

Appendix Two: The Sanctuaries of Sinai

Congregation Sinai
1153 Valencia Street (12th and Valencia)
Los Angeles, CA 90015
Building sold to Welsh Presbyterian Church and still in use by the Church.

Congregation Sinai
3412 West 4th Street (4th and New Hampshire)
Los Angeles, CA 90020
Building currently in use by Korean Philadelphia Presbyterian Church.

Sinai Temple
10400 Wilshire Boulevard (Wilshire and Beverly Glen)
Los Angeles, CA 90024
www.sinaitemple.org
Occupancy since Slichot, 1960.

Appendix Three: The Schools of Sinai Temple

Sinai Akiba Academy
Gesher to 8th grade
Rabbi Laurence Scheindlin, Headmaster

"We introduce students to a life of personal growth, sensitivity, responsibility and intellectual inquiry, shaped by Jewish practices and informed by a respect for diversity of thought."

Douglas Family Early Childhood Center
Ages 2.5 to 5 years old
Tracy Schatz, Director

"The goal of this preschool is to provide an opportunity for the child to develop independence, self-awareness, self-discipline, compassion for others, and a love of learning."

Sinai Temple Religious School (ST*RS)
Kindergarten to 7th grade
Danielle Salem-Kassin, Director

"By the time your children finish the ST*RS program, they will become STARS!"

Appendix Four: The Cemeteries of Sinai*

Mount Sinai Memorial Park/Hollywood Hills
5950 Forest Lawn Drive
Los Angeles, CA 90068

Purchased on March 3, 1964, from Forest Lawn Memorial Park, the Park includes 85 acres in the Hollywood Hills overlooking Burbank, plus its own mortuary. Offers inground burial, aboveground crypts, and kosher crypts.

Mount Sinai Memorial Park/Simi Valley
26150 Mount Sinai Drive
Simi Valley, CA 93063

Dedicated on March 16, 1997, the Park includes 200 acres in the Simi Valley. Mortuary used is Mount Sinai Mortuary at MSMP in Hollywood. Offers in-ground burial, aboveground crypts, and kosher caves. Includes Kamenir Chapel and Ziegler Conference Center.

*Both facilities are established as endowed care trusts, ensuring park maintenance in perpetuity. For further information, please go to: www.mt-sinai.com. Telephone: 1-800-600-0076

Appendix Five: First Board of Directors of Congregation Sinai

J. L. Jonas
Felix Halff
M. Fehr
David Hirsh
Karl Stern
J. Cherman
M. S. Kornblum
J. Rosenberg
M. Cohn
A. Brick
B. Wolff
M. H. Goldstein

Appendix Six: Board of Directors, Sinai Temple, 2006–2007

Jackie Ahdout
Claude Arnall
Norman H. Becker
Shirley Bilfield
Howard Brandes
Linda Camras
Sandy Croll
Eric Diamond
Tom Flesh
Ira M. Friedman
Joseph Gabbaian
Alice Gold
Roz Goldstine
Alan Grushcow
Mark M. Haloossim
Kam Hekmat
David Kekst
Thomas Lane
Aaron Leibovic
David Matloob
Jacob Melamed
Ovvie Miller
Jerry Nagin
Frank Navi
Michael Nazarian
Janet Neman
Ken Nussen
Julie Platt
Lisa Pompan
Jina Rezvanpour
Rick Richman
Gail Rollman
Philip Rosenbaum
Merzad Roshan
Rosa Berman Ruder
Avid Shooshani
Don Shulman
Kurt Smalberg
Anna Tenenblatt
Susan Weisbarth
Joel Weinstein
Terry Wohlberg
Ruth Ziegler, Honorary Life Board Member

Appendix Seven: Sinai Temple Presidents

J. L. Jonas*	1908–1913
J. Laventhal*	1913–1915
Peter R. Haber*	1915–1917
David Hirsh*	1917–1919
Dr. L. G. Reynolds*	1919–1929
Moses Tannenbaum*	1929–1930
Benjamin Platt*	1930–1951
Theodore Strimling*	1951–1953
Edward Hyman*	1953–1955
J. D. Sterling*	1955–1957
Eugene M. Rosen*	1957–1958
Matthew Berman*	1958–1961
Edward Hyman*	1961–1962
Herman Platt*	1962–1964
Allen Ziegler*	1964
Hyman J. Tanenbaum*	1964–1967
Harold Easton*	1967–1969
Dr. Edward Kamenir	1969–1971
Dr. Gerald Freeman	1971–1973
Judge David I. Lippert*	1973–1975
Herman R Friedberg	1975–1977
William Friedland	1977–1979
Doris R. Siegel*	1979–1981
Dr. Max Astrachan*	1981–1982
Aaron Fenton*	1982–1985
M. Milo Mandel	1985–1987
Fred Robin	1987–1989
Dr. Malcolm Cosgrove	1989–1991
Jules Porter	1991–1993
Milton B. Hyman	1993–1995
Judith A. Galperson	1995–1997
Janice L. Zakowski	1997–1999
Jimmy Delshad	1999–2001
Abner D. Goldstine	2001–2003
Brina Rosenbaum	2003–2005
Robert Tom Flesh	2005–2007

*Of Blessed Memory

Appendix Eight: Sinai Temple Sisterhood Presidents*

Mrs. Emil Kornfeld*	1905–1906
Mrs. Kate Peiser*	1906–1907
Mrs. Karl Stern*	1907–1912
Mrs. George Isaacson*	1912–1913
Mrs. Sam Brown*	1913–1915
Mrs. Adolph Sieroty*	1915–1916
Mrs. J. Prelusky*	1916–1917
Mrs. J. B. Mayer*	1917–1918
Mrs. Alberta Levy*	1918–1920
Mrs. Louis G. Reynolds*	1920–1922
Mrs. Eli Elias*	1922–1923
Mrs. David Gordon*	1924–1926
Mrs. Harry Pinko*	1926–1927
Mrs. Samuel Fischgrund*	1927–1928
Mrs. Harry Byrens*	1928–1930
Mrs. Mayer S. Berk*	1930–1932
Mrs. Samuel Markowitz*	1932–1933
Mrs. Louis Tyre*	1933–1935
Mrs. Etta Levinson*	1935–1956
Mrs. Walter Slater Wolff*	1936–1937
Mrs. William Glesby*	1937–1939
Mrs. Jacob Perlman*	1939–1942
Mrs. Charles Roth*	1942–1946
Mrs. Harry Salkin*	1946–1948
Selma Carow-Heuer*	1948–1952
Mrs. Sam Reevin*	1952–1953
Shirley Kirsch	1953–1955
Mrs. Abe Gerstein	1955–1956
Selma Carow-Heuer*	1956–1967
Harriet White	1957–1959
Freddie R. Brown	1959–1960
Ruth Linden	1960–1962
Sylvia Tansey*	1962–1963
Bee Smotrich*	1963–1964
Mae Rubens*	1964–1965
Selma Carow-Heuer*	1965–1966
Violet Friedland	1966–1968
Mildred Tynan*	1968–1970
Evelyn Dreyfuss	1970–1972
Joy Taubman	1972–1974
Arlene Rosenthal	1974–1976
Sandie Lurie	1976–1978
Diane Miller	1978–1980
Dorothy Salkin	1980–1982
Fran Stengel	1982–1984
Joan Karchem	1984–1986
Martha Robin	1986–1988
Frances Katz	1988–1990
Brina Rosenbaum	1990–1992
Doris Pastor	1992–1994
Doris Pastor and Phyllis Dreifus	1994–1995
Jean Powell and Dee Dee Quinn	1996–1997
Dee Dee Quinn	1997–1998
Judith Hoffman	1998–2001
Lila Dwoskin	2001–2002
Carole Greenberg	2002
Jina Rezvanpour	2002–2004
Judith S. Fisher	2004–2006

*Of Blessed Memory

Appendix Nine: Sinai Temple Men's Club Presidents

Reuben Shulman*	1951–1953	Arthur Diamond	1975–1977
Irwin Reiss*	1953–1955	Sidney Katz*	1977–1978
Fred Babbin*	1955–1957	Sol Herzfeld*	1978–1979
Jack Bloom*	1957–1959	Barton Kogan	1979–1980
William Friedland	1959–1961	Abe Guttman	1980–1981
Boris Marks	1961–1962	David Pastor*	1981–1983
Earl Klein	1962–1963	Arthur Perfit*	1983–1984
Irving Tansey*	1963–1964	Norman Karchem	1984–1986
Irving Kory*	1964–1965	Herman Braunstein*	1986–1987
Dr. Samuel Levine	1965–1966	Peter Winkelman	1987–1989
Dr. Mitchell Locks	1966–1967	Donal Dreifus	1989–1991
Norman Atkins	1967–1968	Arthur Omansky	1991–1993
Gerald Berke	1968–1969	Milton Gan*	1993–1995
Jules Porter	1969–1970	Glenn Flug	1995–1996
Murray Rubinow*	1970–1971	Philip Rosenbaum	1996–1999
Ted Levine*	1971–1972	Myles L. Berman	1999–2000
Albert Moscow*	1972–1973	David Matloob	2000–2002
Lee Laine	1973–1974	Stephen Silberman	2002–2004
Ronald Schultz	1974–1975	Joseph Gabbaian	2004–2006

*Of Blessed Memory

Acknowledgments

Many individuals have contributed to the completion of this project. We would like to thank those who volunteered their knowledge, time, and encouragement, and we apologize for any omissions. Thank you to:

- Rabbis David Wolpe, Zvi Dershowitz, Sherre Hirsch, David Lieber, Jacob Pressman, Solomon Rothstein, Allan Schranz, Brian Schuldenfrei, Hillel Silverman
- Cantors Joseph Gole and David Silverstein
- Tom Flesh and the Board of Directors
- Howard Brandes and the Board of Governors
- Carlos Barillos, Frank Fortin, Colin Webb
- Judy Begin, Rebecca Begin, Kay Maurren, Lora Vexler
- Miki Benoff, sculptress, Ner Tamid and Menorahs
- Benjamin Dwoskin and Len Lawrence, Mount Sinai Memorial Park
- Joel Klass at the Jewish Historical Society
- Howard Lesner, Aryell Cohen, Nicholas Mermell, Mike Sirota
- George Shecter, of blessed memory
- Lisa Silverman, Anita Rashtian, and the Library Committee
- Rudy Winkler

Special thanks, also, to all of the other congregants, clergy, staff, and community-at-large who have helped us create a personal glimpse into Sinai Temple's 100-year history.

Photo Credits and Permissions

The photographs used in this history have come from many sources, and, where possible, we have acknowledged the photographer and/or studio. We are sorry for any errors or omissions. Photo credits include:

- Dept. of Special Collections, Charles E. Young Research Library, UCLA *Collection 1429, Los Angeles Times Box 365, Neg#113886. Funeral at Sinai Temple.*
- *The New York Times Copyright © 8/7/60 by the New York Times Co.* Reprinted with permission.
- Jules Porter, Irv Antler, Florie Brizel, Herbert Dallinger, Hallie Lerman, Sol Marshall, Chester Maydole, Nathanson Photographers, Otto Rothschild, Stanart Photo, Witzel Studios.